LET'S COOK IT TOGETHER!

A unique cookery book written especially for par
together.

40p

LET'S COOK IT TOGETHER!

Utterly *SCRUMPTIOUS* Recipes for You and Your Children
—— To Make TOGETHER — Vegetarian Style! ——

by
Peggy Brusseau

Illustrated by Vincent Driver

THORSONS PUBLISHING GROUP
Wellingborough, Northamptonshire
———— • ————
Rochester, Vermont

First published 1986

British Library Cataloguing in Publication Data

Brusseau, Peggy
  Let's cook it together!: utterly scrumptious
  recipes for adults and children — vegetarian
  style.
  1. Vegetarian cookery
  I. Title
  641.5'636   TX837

  ISBN 0-7225-1299-6

Printed and bound in Great Britain

CONTENTS

DEDICATION

This book is dedicated to families.

ACKNOWLEDGEMENTS

My deepest gratitude to Peter, who brews infectious laughter, cooks addictive optimism and always tells me what his taste buds are thinking.

Love and thanks to my Mother and Father for their patience and persistence when I was learning.

And thanks to Valerie for sharing her kitchen.

HELLO AND WELCOME TO THE FUN!

Traditionally, the kitchen has always been right at the heart of family life. But, sadly, these days many families don't seem to be able to spend much time together, just having fun. This book aims to put the shared fun and togetherness back where it belongs in family life — no matter whether you happen to be a working parent, a stay-at-home parent, a single parent or even a grandparent.

Apart from having lots of fun and excitement while you prepare these meatless recipes together, you'll also be sharing the kitchen workload more fairly, and be producing some delicious mealtime treats too! And all the time, you'll be helping your children to establish a healthy, skillful, and social interest in food (just like the way it used to be!).

HOW TO USE THE BOOK

There's no need to work methodically through each section, just pick any recipe that sounds attractive to everyone, and begin. Each recipe is arranged to show how food preparation may be shared between parents and children. The 🐱 symbol denotes the parent's activities (always in the column on the left) and the 🐱 symbol shows those for the children (in the right hand column). The recipes are separated into stages by lines across the page, and generally both parents and children will have jobs to do simultaneously (this speeds up preparation time).

As you look through this book you will see that in some recipes the child uses a knife, for instance, in others nothing more dangerous than a spoon. You may want to bear this safety factor in mind when selecting dishes to prepare with very young children who are inexperienced with kitchen utensils. If you are working with more than one child, or children of different ages, then you may have to give them some of *your* jobs (under supervision, of course).

The preparation times given are approximate: a family really experienced in working together may find they have completed the preparations 10 minutes earlier than stated. Families new to co-operative cooking may wish to allow 10 minutes more. It is true that the more together you become, the faster you work.

You will be amazed how quickly children acquire new skills when they are having a good time. Learning cookery skills gradually, with your full support and in an atmosphere of fun will help your children to develop confidence, healthy eating habits and sensible, *safe* use of kitchen equipment.

Speaking of which, any special equipment necessary to prepare a dish is placed at the end of the list of ingredients. Otherwise, the ingredients are named in the order of use.

Each recipe has an introduction explaining the history of the dish, or the reason for its title. In some of these introductions, stories and questions are included which may be used as fun and fascinating diversions if the excitement gets too much or, perhaps, if there are too many children to allow all of them to participate. They provide plenty of scope for children who wish to sit quietly drawing, reading or imagining while the meal is prepared around them. And they can help to turn a conversation away from 'who-gets-to-do-what' onto matters of greater interest and fewer decibels!

SOME HINTS ON INGREDIENTS

You may not have cooked meatless meals before, or you may find you are unfamiliar with some of the ingredients listed in these recipes. So I'd like to mention just a few of them. They are all easily acquired and good value for money with the added bonus of being healthy. You will be able to purchase most of these ingredients at a good local supermarket, or whole food shop.

SOYA OIL: This oil contains a substance (linoleic acid) which our bodies need in order to utilize the nutrients in our food. Corn oil contains the same amount, but I found the flavour didn't suit all of these recipes. A good substitute is cold-pressed safflower or sunflower oil. It is more expensive, has a strong but pleasing flavour, and even more linoleic acid. I recommend that you *do not* use oil that is just mysteriously labelled 'Vegetable Oil'.

MARGARINE or BUTTER: You must decide which you prefer. I use *Granose* or *Vitaquel* vegetable margarines. Both are free from milk products and colouring. If you choose to use butter, you may purchase brands that are both unsalted and uncoloured.

CHEESE: I use 'vegetarian' cheeses when possible. These are made without animal rennet (a substance which curdles milk and is derived from the stomach of unweaned calves) and are usually marketed as such. If you are uncertain whether a cheese is 'vegetarian' or not, ask in the shop or write to the manufacturer. Some of these recipes include cheese such as Parmesan, which is unlikely to be 'vegetarian'. You must decide whether you wish to prepare the recipe as written. If you do not wish to use cheese at all, then tofu (soya bean cheese) is a delicious substitute.

MILK: SOYA or COW'S: Soya milk is made from the soya bean. It is a nutritious, tasty milk that is easily purchased, and easy to make at home. If you decide to make it yourself, you can produce many pints for just a few pennies. It may be purchased ready to drink, in concentrate or dried. Those who consume no animal products whatsoever may find this milk becomes an important part of their diet (if this applies to you make sure it is fortified). There are few allergies associated with soya milk, but it should not be given to very young children (under one year of age).

Cow's milk is also nutritious and very easily acquired. Because it is animal derived, there are diseases associated with meat foods which may be transmitted through it (eg., salmonella). And there are certainly some allergic reactions ascribed to it, such as asthma, eczema and colic in children.

I personally choose soya milk in preference to cow's milk. I really enjoy the taste, I find it versatile in cooking, inexpensive and fun to make. I get my quota of cow's milk when I have a piece of cheese.

EGGS: Many supermarkets now sell free-range eggs. These are preferable to battery eggs not only in terms of taste but because they are obtained through a less cruel form of production. If you do not eat eggs, I recommend that you substitute 1 tablespoon of tahini (sesame seed paste) for each egg listed in these recipes.

SALT: I do not add salt while cooking unless it is necessary (eg., to remove the 'bitter' juices from aubergines). If salt is included or recommended as a condiment, then sea salt is preferable as it is unrefined and contains a variety of minerals useful to our body function. Alternatively, you could use Tamari or Shoyu (both genuinely fermented soya sauce, not the mass produced concoction), although they do contain sodium.

RICE: I always use a variety of brown, whole grain rice. It is nutty in flavour and very nutritious. Occasionally, I use Basmati rice. This is lighter in colour than brown rice and may be mistaken for refined and polished — it is neither. Both brown and basmati rice may be acquired organically grown which tends to further improve their flavour.

ORGANIC FOODS: are those which have been grown without chemical pesticides, fertilizers, hormones or other additives. They are safer, tastier and contain more nutrients. Health food shops as well as some greengrocers supply them in season, and an increasing number of supermarkets are starting to sell them, too. Alternatively, you may have an allotment or a strip of garden suitable for growing your own organic vegetables. They are definitely of higher quality — I prefer them every time.

I hope this book will encourage you to enjoy the pleasures of cooking together with your family. I wish you skill, health and fun.

And now......Let's Get Cooking!

Peggy Brusseau

9

1. SOUPS

BEAVER'S DAM SOUP

Beavers are otter-like animals with big front teeth that live in the lakes and rivers of Canada and northern United States. They are superb engineers, and very industrious and ambitious builders. They make their own homes (including secret underwater entrances) and also build huge dams across rivers and lakes. The tangle of branches and twigs they use for building is just like the tangle of herbs and beansprouts in this soup, which is best in late summer when the parsley and tarragon are fresh. It will serve 2 adults and 2 children and takes only 20 minutes to prepare and cook.

1 litre (approx. 2 pints) of water	55g (2oz) of fresh tarragon
10ml (2 teaspoons) yeast extract	55g (2oz) of mung beansprouts
55g (2oz) of fresh parsley	55g (2oz) of alfalfa seed sprouts

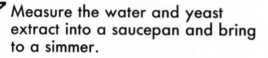
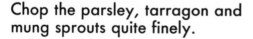

Measure the water and yeast extract into a saucepan and bring to a simmer.	Wash the parsley, tarragon and beansprouts.
Chop the parsley, tarragon and mung sprouts quite finely.	Put both kinds of sprouts into a large mixing bowl and stir well with your hands.
	Add the herbs to the beansprouts and continue stirring with your hands.
Add the herb and beansprout mixture to the stock and remove the soup from the heat. Stir well and cover the saucepan.	
Prepare the soup bowls and serve the soup immediately.	

METAMORPHOSIS SOUP

A metamorphosis is something that happens to tadpoles when they change into frogs ... hopefully, this soup won't change *you* into a frog, unless you happen to be a prince or princess in a fairy-tale, so you never know! There are ploppy green things in it to remind you of frogs (actually, they're courgettes and are difficult to keep on your spoon) and black peppercorns to look like tadpoles. Of course, no nice person would ever think of eating a real frog. Do you know the difference between a frog and a toad? And can you think of any other animals that undergo metamorphosis? (See end of recipe). Have a think while you're making this recipe, which makes enough for 2 adults and 2 children, and takes 50 minutes to prepare.

2 small courgettes 1 litre (approx. 2 pints) of water 15ml (1 tablespoon) of sea salt 140g (5oz) of tomato purée 15ml (1 tablespoon) of tamari	12 whole peppercorns 5ml (1 teaspoon) of dried basil (or ½ oz fresh) 15ml (1 tablespoon) soya oil

Wash and trim the courgettes and slice them in half along their length.	Measure out the water and pour into a saucepan.
Place the courgettes on a plate with the sliced side up. Sprinkle them liberally with the salt, put to one side.	Add the tomato purée to the water and stir. Add the tamari to the water.
Place the tomato mixture over a medium heat and bring to a simmer.	Add the peppercorns and basil to the saucepan.
When the courgettes have salted for 25 minutes, wash them thoroughly in cold water. Now cut them into diagonal chunks (frogs) and sauté them in the soya oil for 5 minutes.	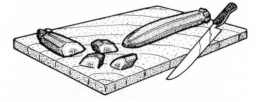
	Add to the courgette 'frogs' to the tomato 'pond' and stir well.

Allow the soup to simmer for another 20 minutes. Serve immediately with plenty of bread. Leave the peppercorns on the bottom of the bowl.

Frogs leap and hop while toads, who have shorter legs, must be content to walk. Also, frogs are smooth-skinned and need to be close to water or damp places – toads are often warty and may be found far from water.

A caterpillar undergoes a metamorphosis into an insect – like a butterfly.

BIG YAWN SOUP

Lettuce is said to be soporific – which means it makes you feel sleepy. Sleep is very good for you and if you don't get enough of it you may find yourself having a 'micro sleep' which lasts only a second and can occur at any time of day. People spend about one third of their lives asleep and part of that time dreaming, when, of course, anything can happen ... What did *you* dream about last night? This soup needs only 25 minutes for preparation and cooking. It serves 2 adults and 2 children.

1 litre (approx. 2 pints) of water 1 whole cos lettuce	2.5ml ($\frac{1}{2}$ teaspoon) of nutmeg 1 orange

Boil the water in a saucepan.	Wash the lettuce and trim the leaves.
Slice the lettuce into very thin strips: 6mm ($\frac{1}{4}$ inch) wide.	
Measure the nutmeg and add to the water.	Add the sliced lettuce to the saucepan and stir well.
Simmer the soup for 10 minutes.	Slice the orange in half.
Squeeze the orange juice into the soup and remove it from the heat.	Prepare the soup bowls.

Stir the soup well and serve it immediately with Re-Baked Bread (page 72). Then go have a nap or a big sleep.

DANDELION AT NOON

This soup is especially attractive, and viewed from the top resembles a dandelion flower when it is fully open at noon on a sunny day. The bright yellow colour of the soup represents the dandelion flower, the cucumber slices look like its leaves, and the lettuce which overhangs the bowl is the surrounding green meadow. 'Dandelion' comes from the French 'dent de lion', meaning lion's tooth (look at the rough edges of its leaves and you'll see why). Although there are no real dandelions in this soup, people in England have used them for hundreds of years, as a herb and as a vegetable in salads (see who can produce the longest list of other herbs – from memory). This recipe will feed 2 adults and 2 children, and takes 40 minutes to prepare, including cooking.

1 whole cauliflower
15ml (1 tablespoon) of whole wheat flour
5ml (1 teaspoon) of ground coriander
15ml (1 tablespoon) of butter or polyunsaturated margarine

570 ml (1 pint) of milk (soya or cow's)
570ml (1 pint) of water
7.5ml (1½ teaspoons) of turmeric
½ of a cucumber
¼ of a lettuce
A hand mouli

Remove the outer leaves from a cauliflower and cut the florets from the stalk. Place them in a colander. Cut the stalk into small strips and place these in the colander also. Rinse well and drain.

Measure the flour and coriander into a small bowl. Stir well.

Measure the butter or margarine into a saucepan and place over a low heat.

Pour the milk into a jug with the water.

When the butter has melted, stir in the turmeric.

Wash the cucumber.

Gradually add the flour and coriander mix to the butter and turmeric, stirring to make a roux.

Slice the cucumber into rounds about 6mm (¼ inch) thick.

As the roux thickens, add small amounts of the milk and water mixture. Stir very well between each addition.

Now cut each round into halves. Place these to one side.

When all of the liquid is used, add the cauliflower pieces and cover the pan. Allow the soup to simmer for about 20 minutes.

Wash one quarter of a lettuce. Select the soup bowls.

Slice the lettuce into thin, lacey strips and place them in the bowls. The lettuce should cover the bottom of the bowls and overhang the sides.

Find the hand mouli and prepare the coarse sieve for use.

When the cauliflower is tender, take the soup from the heat and ladle it into the mouli.

Turn the handle so the soup is pushed through into a tureen.

Stir the cucumber strips into the puréed soup.

Ladle the soup over the lettuce and serve immediately.

ROYAL DECREE SOUP

Have you ever wondered how people used to measure things long ago, in the days before rulers and tape measures were invented? One way was to count the number of paces it took you to cover the ground you wanted to measure. Another way, for smaller measurements, was to count the number of hand 'spans'. But neither of these worked very well, because different people have lots of different sizes of pace and hand spans. Can you imagine what confusion *that* created? To try and improve things, the English King Edward the Second issued a Royal Decree in 1324 that standardized the 'inch' as three barley grains, and the 'foot' as 39 barley grains placed end to end, and this soup celebrates that Royal Decree. Serve it in bright blue or yellow bowls to set off its subtle colours. Cook the barley in a stainless steel or enamel pan as iron can sometimes cause it to discolour. Allow 40 minutes cooking time. The amount serves 2 adults and 2 children.

225g (8 oz) of barley	15ml (1 tablespoon) of soya oil
3.5 litres (6 pints) of water	2 large onions
1 whole celery	2 bay-leaves

Wash the barley and place in a saucepan with the water. Boil, then reduce the heat and simmer.	Wash all of the celery – leaves and stalks. You may have to scrub the stalks with a small vegetable brush.
Measure the soya oil into a small frying pan.	Chop the celery stalks into thin chunks. Put the leaves aside.
Peel and chop the onions quite finely. Add them to the oil in the frying pan and sauté over a gentle heat.	Chop the celery leaves finely. Wash the bay-leaves.
When the barley has cooked for 20 minutes, add the sautéed onions and stir well.	Add the bay-leaves and celery to the barley and stir well.
Allow the soup to simmer for approximately 10 minutes more.	Add the celery leaves and stir.
Cover the soup and remove it from the heat.	Prepare the soup bowls.
Serve immediately, in bright-coloured bowls, with a garnish of celery leaves.	

VEGETABLE STOCK

Real vegetable stock adds a depth and texture to any soup you make (though you can substitute yeast extract, vegetable extract or vegetable stock cubes). It is very economical, convenient and satisfying to make. Prepare it while you are making other dishes so that you may add the peelings, stalks and odd-bits to the broth. You may prefer to *save* things like broccoli stalks and ends of celery, in which case just wash them and put them in your freezer until you next make this stock. You can also strain the stock of all solids and then freeze it in ice-cube trays for easy use later. Just tip a frozen litre of cubes into your saucepan when you next prepare one of the following recipes. In this recipe, the onion peel is added to give a lovely amber colour to the stock. Allow one hour to prepare and cook approximately 4 litres of stock.

4.5 litres (approx. 8 pints) of water 3 large potatoes (peel and/ or flesh 680g (1½lb) of root vegetables (carrots, parsnips, swedes) 2 large onions	2 outside leaves of greens The heart of 1 cabbage 2 bay-leaves The leaf and white end of 1 celery 55g (2oz) of rice or barley

Measure the water into a large saucepan over a low heat.	Scrub the potatoes and roots.
Peel and chop the onion. Add *both* the peel and flesh to the saucepan.	Wash the greens and cabbage.
Chop the potatoes and roots and add them to the saucepan.	Wash the bay-leaves and add them to the stock.
	Slice or chop the greens and the cabbage, add to the stock.
Wash the celery and chop it.	Add the celery to the stock.
Rinse the rice or barley in very cold water.	Add the rice or barley to the stock and stir very well.

Simmer the stock for a further 45 minutes. Strain it of all solids and use it immediately or freeze it in pre-measured amounts.

SUMMER LAKES SOUP

My home state of Minnesota is called 'the land of ten thousand lakes'. Every summer a thick layer of algae grows on the surface of these lakes, making them look like huge bowls of soup. In *this* soup the parsley and watercress float to the top, just like the algae. The bay-leaf reminds me of a lilypad, and the carrot looks like sunfish swimming about. It takes 30 minutes to prepare, including cooking time, and serves 2 adults and 2 children.

2 litres (approx. 4 pints) of vegetable stock *55g (2oz) of fresh parsley* *55g (2oz) of fresh watercress*	*1 medium onion* *1 large carrot* *4 small bay-leaves* *A vegetable peeler*

Prepare 2 litres (4 pints of vegetable broth (see the recipe on page 17) and bring the broth to a slow simmer.

Wash and chop the parsley and the watercress – you may include the thin stalks too. Add these to the broth and stir.

Slice the onion into very thin rings and add to the broth.

Flip a coin to see who gets to scrub the carrot.

Use the vegetable peeler to slice the whole carrot into long, thin strips. Add them to the broth.

The loser gets to wash the bay-leaves.

Let the soup simmer for 10 minutes.

Set out the soup bowls.

Remove the soup from the heat and ladle the soup into the bowls.

Garnish each serving with one of the bay-leaves.

Serve immediately.

GENGHIS KHAN BROTH

This soup is named after one of the most powerful people in the history of the world – the mighty tyrant Genghis Khan, who ruled the Mongol tribes until the early thirteenth century. It's called after him because he would have been sure to have tasted both its main ingredients as he dominated the world from the Sea of Japan in the East to the Mediterranean in the West. On his travels, he would have come across the orange (grown first in China, from about 2500 B.C.) and the asparagus (originating from the cold and bitter Russian steppes). It takes only 30 minutes to make from beginning to end (sometimes that *includes* the eating!) and provides enough for 1 Genghis Khan, or 2 adults and 2 children.

225g (8oz) of fresh asparagus 2 small oranges	1 litre (approx. 2 pints) of vegetable stock $\frac{1}{2}$ of a cucumber
Wash the asparagus and scrape the lower portion of each spear.	Wash the oranges and cut them into halves.
Measure the stock into a saucepan.	Chop the 'spears' into 2.5cm (1 inch) long chunks.
Bring the liquid to a fast simmer and add the asparagus chunks.	Wash the cucumber.
Slice one of the orange halves into four slices.	Chop the cucumber into four 2.5cm (1 inch) thick pieces.
Stir the soup often, each time pressing the asparagus pieces to the side of the pan.	Squeeze the remaining three orange halves and put the juice to one side.
	Place one slice of orange and one piece of cucumber in each soup bowl.
Remove the soup from the heat after 20 minutes and add the orange juice. Stir well.	
Ladle the soup over the orange and cucumber slices. Serve immediately.	

POT BELLY SOUP

This soup is so good you won't want to stop eating it, which is why it's called 'Pot Belly Soup'! It's a hearty winter soup, good for warming up after a trek in the snow, and is just what the early Western trailblazers kept slowly simmering over their log fires, all day long. It's delicious with a slice of freshly baked crusty bread. It takes just 15 minutes to prepare and 30 minutes to cook, although it will improve with slow cooking. It makes enough for 2 adults and 2 children.

900g (2lb) of potatoes 15ml (1 tablespoon) of soya oil 455g (1lb) of leeks 2 litres (approx. 4 pints) of vegetable stock 4 cloves of garlic	10ml (2 teaspoons) of fennel seed 10ml (2 teaspoons) of freshly ground black pepper 55g (2oz) of bran 30g (1oz) of brewer's yeast 30ml (2 tablespoons) of tamari

Wash and chop the potatoes. Place them in a large saucepan with the soya oil.	Wash and trim the leeks.
Sauté the potatoes over a medium heat for 5 minutes. Stir often.	Carefully slice the leeks into thin circles and put to one side.
Add some of the vegetable stock to the saucepan and stir.	Peel the garlic cloves. Add them to the soup.
Add the leeks and the remaining stock to the saucepan. Stir.	Measure out the fennel seeds and add to the soup.
Sprinkle the black pepper into the soup.	Weigh out the bran and add it to the soup.
Add the brewer's yeast to the soup and stir well.	Pour the tamari into the broth and stir.

Allow the soup to cook for 10 minutes longer, then serve immediately.

A B C SOUP

'A is for Apple, B is for Beans, C is for Cinnamon straight from its tree.' This soup has all three of those ingredients to make a delicate, scented broth that will serve 2 adults and 2 children. You will need 45 minutes to cook it and a bit of forethought to prepare the beans. Idea: can you finish the alphabet of food?

225g (8oz) of dried soya beans *680g (1½lb)of cooking apples* *1.5 litres (3 pints) of vegetable stock*	*1 whole stick of cinnamon* *A pressure cooker*

Measure the soya beans into a bowl and wash them well in cold water. Now cover them in clean, cold water and leave them to soak overnight or for 6–8 hours.

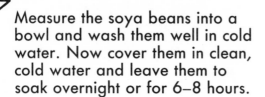

Wash the cooking apples and remove their stems.

Drain the beans and place them in the pressure cooker with a little water. Cook them for 20 minutes at pressure.

Peel, quarter and core the apples. Slice each quarter into small chunks.

Measure the stock into a large saucepan.

Place the stock over a medium heat and add the chopped apples. When the beans have cooked, add them to the stock.

Break the cinnamon stick into four pieces and add these to the stock. Stir well.

Allow the soup to simmer for another 10 minutes then serve immediately. Ensure that one piece of cinnamon is included in each serving.

PAUL BUNYAN'S TEARS

A lumberjack is a tough woodsman with muscles of iron and a bottomless appetite! Paul Bunyan is a giant lumberjack who lives in the wild north country of Minnesota, with his only friend Babe, the Blue Ox. Every time he takes a step his huge footprint fills with water and becomes an enormous lake. In winter it gets so cold up there that all the words he speaks freeze as soon as he says them (so the winter is very quiet). But each spring the words thaw out and sound all at once, like incredible booming thunderclaps. And sometimes, being the only giant for hundreds of miles around, he gets so lonely that he cries – causing great floods that sweep the woods, the timber and everything else away with them. This soup recreates one of these floods – the broth represents his tears, the carrots and parsnips are bits of timber, the chunks of potato are small pieces of ice not yet melted, the caraway are uprooted plants and bushes. There is enough here for 2 hungry adults and 2 hungry children. This will take 50 minutes in all – preparation and cooking.

15ml (1 tablespoon) of soya oil 3 large potatoes 3 large parsnips 3 large carrots 1 large onion	10ml (2 teaspoons) of caraway seed 2 litres (approx. 4 pints) of vegetable stock 15ml (1 tablespoon) of yeast extract

Measure the soya oil into a large saucepan and place over a low heat.	Scrub the potatoes, parsnips and carrots really well.
Peel and chop the onion and add to the oil. Stir often to sauté.	Chop the potatoes into small chunks – leave the peel on.
'Top and tail' the parsnips and the carrots and slice them into long, thin pieces. Add them to the onion.	Add the potato chunks to the onion in the saucepan.
Turn the heat up and stir the onion and vegetable mix constantly.	Measure the caraway seed.
	When the vegetables have browned slightly, add the vegetable stock to the saucepan. Stir well.

Add the caraway seed and the yeast extract to the soup. Stir and leave to simmer for about 30 minutes.

Ladle this soup into deep bowls and serve immediately.

DRAGON'S TOOTH SOUP

Every year a dragon grows a new tooth, and throws away the old one. If you're clever enough to pick these up and make a soup out of them, you'll become invisble, invincible, incorrigible and totally incomprehensible too. If you are short on dragon's teeth, use a dozen almonds and a dozen garlic cloves instead (don't worry, when the garlic is cooked it tastes very mild, not at all like dragon's breath). Allow 30 minutes to cook enough for 2 adults and 2 children.

A little boiling water *12 whole almonds* *1 medium swede* *12 cloves of garlic*	*1 large onion* *15ml (1 tablespoon) of soya oil* *1.7 litres (3 pints) of vegetable stock*

Pour a little boiling water over the whole almonds. Their skins will shrivel.	Peel and wash the swede. Peel the garlic cloves.
Peel, then chop the onion very finely. Sauté in the soya oil.	Measure the stock into a saucepan and bring to a simmer.
Grate the swede.	Peel the almonds and add them to the stock.
Add the sautéed onion and the whole garlic to the stock.	Add the grated swede to the soup and stir well.
Prepare the soup bowls.	

Simmer the soup for 15 minutes more then serve immediately.

GREEN LACE FRUIT SALAD

This salad looks green and delicate, just like green lace (you've probably never heard of green lace *or* thought of combining peppers and cucumbers with fruit – but it works!) It has a luscious and refreshing flavour, which is enhanced by its minty dressing, and is sure to get you hooked. The preparation takes 30 minutes for 4 servings (2 adults and 2 children).

2 green eating apples	15g (½oz) fresh mint leaves
225g (½lb) of green grapes	30ml (2 tablespoons) of honey
1 green pepper	15ml (1 tablespoon) of
15g (½oz) fresh coriander leaves	cider vinegar
	½ of a cucumber

Quarter the apples, core them and slice them finely along the length of the apple.	Wash the grapes and take them off their stalks. Now slice each one in half.
Wash the pepper and slice it into rings, removing the pulp.	Wash the coriander leaves and remove their stalks.
Wash and chop the mint leaves and place them in a jug with the honey and vinegar. Stir very well with a fork.	Slice the cucumber into thin circles.

Arrange the fruits on a large plate. Start on the outside edge of the plate and work in circles going towards the centre: green peppers, green apples, coriander leaves, cucumber circles, green grapes, more coriander leaves, cucumber and grapes. The fruits should overlap slightly to give the effect of lace.

Now pour the mint and honey dressing over all and serve.

NEEDLES IN A HAYSTACK

This sturdy, late-summer salad is made of finely shredded vegetables tossed together to form the 'haystack', and the 'needles' are the crunchy slivers of celery. Real needles can be dangerous if you lose them, because they are sharp and might prick you. Can you think of a good way to find a *real* needle without it hurting? (See bottom of page for answer). You will need 30 minutes to prepare enough for 2 adults and 2 children.

¼ of a white cabbage 1 large onion 2 large carrots 1 medium turnip ½ of a crisp lettuce	115g (4oz) fresh watercress 2 stalks of celery 5ml (1 teaspoon) poppy seed 5ml (1 teaspoon) celery seed

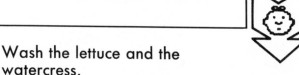

Wash, trim and grate the cabbage, onion, carrots and turnip.	Wash the lettuce and the watercress.
Thinly slice the lettuce and watercress and toss the vegetables together into a 'haystack'.	Wash the celery and chop the thick ends off. Cut each stalk into four chunks.
Carefully slice each chunk of celery into long, thin 'needles'.	Add the 'needles' to the 'haystack'. Sprinkle the poppy and celery seeds over all.

Toss the salad one final time and serve it with your favourite dressing (see pages 94–104 for some dressing ideas).

Answer: use a magnet.

25

FAERIES' GLEN SALAD

Some people think that faeries are imaginary but this salad will enchant you into thinking otherwise. You must arrange it carefully to show the sort of place a faerie would live: lush meadows, hills, paths and clusters of mushrooms. Just to convince you, next time you're out walking, look for faerie-rings in the grass (you can tell them because they are a brighter green); they are the marks left after a faerie dance. You might even see some faerie-money, which has the unfortunate habit of turning into withered leaves and blowing away – just when you thought you might grab hold of it. This takes about 30 minutes to prepare and will serve 4.

4 large flat mushrooms	*115g (4oz) of natural yogurt*
½ of an iceberg lettuce	*5ml (1 teaspoon) of paprika*
225g (8oz) of ripe tomatoes	*1 ripe avocado*
1 small green pepper	*A large serving plate*
1 medium onion	*A china or plastic faerie*

Trim the mushroom stalks and rub clean or peel their heads.	Wash the lettuce and shake off the excess water.
Slice the lettuce into very fine shreds.	Wash the tomatoes and the green pepper.
Peel and thinly slice the onion and mix with the shredded lettuce.	
Slice the tomatoes very thinly.	Spread the lettuce and onion onto the serving plate: this is lush meadow with flowers.
Cut the green pepper into quarters along its length. Remove the stalk and the pulp.	Measure the yogurt into a small bowl. Add the paprika and stir well.
Cut the avocado in half and remove the pip. Carefully peel each half and cut in half again lengthwise.	Place the mushrooms in a cluster on the serving plate.
Place the quarters of avocado and green pepper alternately in a group opposite the mushrooms: these are hills, so make sure their rounded sides are uppermost.	

Place the slices of tomato in a 'path' from the mushrooms to the 'hills' (the slices should overlap slightly).

Carefully pour the yogurt and paprika mixture along either side of the 'path' – just like cow-parsley or wild elder.

Place the little faerie under the mushrooms, at the beginning of the 'path'.

Serve this with your favourite dressing (see pages 94–104 for more dressing ideas) or more of the yogurt and paprika mixture. Be certain that each serving has one whole mushroom and its own portion of avocado, green pepper and tomato.

VERDI PRESTO SALAD

This salad is the quickest, tastiest way I know to get the goodness of greens into every mouth in the house – that's why it's called 'presto'. The slightly bitter taste of spinach is enhanced and disguised at once by the sweetness of lettuce. Both are sliced into lacey-thin strips to prevent toughness, doused in the simple sauce, tossed together and – presto – there it is. Allow 20 minutes preparation time. This will serve 2 adults and 2 children.

1 large onion 115g (4oz) of fresh spinach 115g (4oz) of crisp lettuce	45ml (3 tablespoons) olive oil 45ml (3 tablespoons) cider vinegar 2 cloves of garlic

Peel and thinly slice the onion.	Wash the spinach and lettuce and shake the excess water from them.
Slice the spinach into thin strips and trim the stems away. Slice the lettuce into strips also and mix them together in a serving bowl.	Measure the olive oil and the vinegar into a small saucepan.
Place the oil and vinegar over a low heat. Peel the garlic cloves, crush them and add them to the saucepan.	Add the sliced onion to the saucepan.
When the oil and vinegar have come to a fast simmer, remove the pan from the heat and allow the mix to cool until tepid.	
	Pour the mixture over the spinach and lettuce. Stir the salad very well.

Serve immediately in wooden salad bowls.

PRESERVATION SALAD

Drying food is probably the oldest method of food preservation known, and this salad can be made from ingredients which have all been preserved in this manner (even the onion could be dried, but fresh would be better, and the peas can be canned). This means you can eat it absolutely all year round! It can be eaten as a meal in itself, or as part of a larger buffet. It will also keep well in the refrigerator (cover it to make sure it doesn't take on the flavour of other things in the fridge). Can you think of other ways of preserving food? The salad takes 45 minutes to prepare – including cooking time for the millet. It will serve 2 adults and 2 children.

170g (6oz) of millet 570ml (1 pint) of boiling water 170g (6oz) of peas 1 small onion	115g (4oz) of whole or ground unsalted peanuts 5ml (1 teaspoon) of paprika 2.5ml (½ teaspoon) of ground ginger

Wash the millet. Place in a saucepan with the boiling water. Bring to a simmer.	Wash the peas.
Peel and finely chop the onion.	Measure the peanuts into a large salad bowl. Add the peas and the chopped onion.
Stir the millet. Allow it to simmer for 15–20 minutes.	Measure the paprika and ginger into the salad mixture.
When the millet is tender to chew, drain the liquid from it and rinse it under cold water. Allow it to drain thoroughly.	
	Add the cool, cooked millet to the salad bowl. Give one final stir to mix all ingredients.
Serve immediately with a dressing of your choice.	

CAPILLARY ACTION SALAD

This salad is an edible scientific experiment, which will show you how trees and other vegetation take water all the way from their deepest roots right up to the top of their branches by capillary action. Fill a tall jug with water that has been coloured by cooking beetroot in it. Now place the sticks of celery in the water for 30–60 mins. When you come back the celery will have brightly coloured veins.

This salad will take 30 minutes to prepare, after you've finished the experiment, but may improve with being chilled for an hour or so. This will serve 2 adults and 2 children.

1 large beetroot 570ml (1 pint) of water 1 head of fresh celery 285ml (½ pint) of wine vinegar	225g (½lb) of fresh broad beans 455g (1lb) of fresh tomatoes 15g (½oz) of fresh mint 10ml (2 teaspoons) of mustard seed

Simmer one sliced beetroot in 570ml (1 pint) of water until the beetroot is tender and the water a deep red. Allow the water to cool slightly.	Wash the celery stalks and put the leaves to one side.
Pour the beetroot water into a deep jug (place the cooked beetroot aside).	Immerse the celery stalks in the jug of beetroot water.
Measure the wine vinegar into a small, deep bowl.	Pod the broad beans.
Steam the broad beans until just tender. Add them to the vinegar.	Wash the tomatoes and remove their stems.
Wash the mint and chop it finely.	Measure the mustard seed.
Cut the tomatoes into quarters and remove any pieces of core. Place the tomatoes in a large bowl.	Place the beans, vinegar, mint and mustard seed into the large bowl with the tomatoes.
Chop the red-veined celery into the bowl with the other vegetables. Mix them really well.	

Cover and chill for an hour, or serve immediately.

BOTANISTS' SALAD

Botanists study plant life – they know every part of a plant's structure: roots, leaves, stems, flowers, seeds and fruit. This salad has all of those parts, but from different plants. Here's an idea – draw a completely new, crazy plant made from the ingredients in this salad. Now give that plant an even crazier name. This takes 30 minutes to prepare and will feed 2 adults and 2 children.

1 large beetroot $\frac{1}{4}$ of a whole red cabbage 15g ($\frac{1}{2}$oz) of fresh parsley 4 stalks of celery	7–15g ($\frac{1}{4}$–$\frac{1}{2}$oz) of marigold petals 115g (4 oz) of currants or sultanas 55g (2oz) of pumpkin seeds

Scrub the beetroot and then top and tail it. Grate it through a coarse serration.	Wash the red cabbage.
Chop the cabbage and place, with the beetroot, in a large bowl.	Wash the parsley and chop it finely. Add it to the other plants in the salad bowl.
Wash the celery and chop finely. Add these to the large bowl.	Measure the marigold petals and put aside.
Measure out the currants and pick them over for any stems or twigs. Add these to the salad.	Measure out the pumpkin seeds and rinse them under cool water. Drain them and add them to the salad.

Stir the salad very well. Sprinkle the marigold petals over the top of the salad just before serving. Serve with the dressing of your choice.

SUNRISE SALAD

You needn't *eat* this at sunrise, although that would be appropriate. The ingredients are arranged into a picture of sunrise – complete with mist and haze. This salad is refreshing for lunch or as a dessert to a heavier meal. It will serve 2 adults and 2 children and takes 20 minutes to prepare. Do you know: what sort of a clock only works after sunrise?

1 large grapefruit	2 large oranges
2 red eating apples	55g (2oz) of natural yogurt
2 green eating apples	30ml (2 tablespoons) of honey
2 ripe bananas	A large serving plate

Peel the grapefruit and break it into sections. Set them aside.

Wash the apples.

Quarter, core and slice the apples along their length into thin slices.

Peel the bananas and slice each one in half along its length.

Peel the oranges and break them into segments.

Spread the green apples out along the bottom of the serving plate, each slice slightly overlapping. This is the horizon.

Place the grapefruit sections above the horizon, right in the centre. This is the sun itself, so make it round.

Place each banana half so that one end just touches the grapefruit 'sun' and the other end reaches away from its centre. These are sun-rays.

Place red apple slices along both sides of each banana half, running lengthwise with the red peel nearest to the banana.

Fill up the spaces in between the red apples with orange segments, also running lengthwise.

Pour the yogurt over the green apple 'horizon'. That is to be the early morning mist.

Pour the honey across the sun and its rays. That is to be the sunrise haze.

This may be chilled briefly but is best served at once.

Answer: a sundial.

SAILORS' MARINADE

The start of the sixteenth century marked the beginning of the great long-distance sea voyages, from Europe to North and South America, Africa and Asia. Interestingly, most of their great discoveries were made by mistake – such as Columbus, who, happening upon Cuba off the American coast in 1493, thought that he had discovered a new route to China! One of the great problems the seafarers faced was spending many months at sea without being able to eat fresh vegetables – causing them to suffer from diseases, in particular scurvy, which results from lack of Vitamin C (only found in fruit and vegetables). Eventually, all the housewives on land put their skill to work to find methods of preserving fruit and vegetables to send to sea with their men. A barrel full of a marinade like this would have pleased the whole crew for many weeks – and kept them healthy. This will take 1 hour to prepare. Enough here for 8 servings.

170g (6oz) of baby onions	16 baby ears of sweet corn
225g ($\frac{1}{2}$lb) of baby carrots	12 whole peppercorns
285ml ($\frac{1}{2}$ pint) of cider vinegar	115g (4oz) of baby French beans
140ml ($\frac{1}{4}$ pint) of olive (or soya) oil	115g (4oz) of baby peas

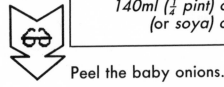

Peel the baby onions.	Scrub the baby carrots and slice the tops from them.
Pour the vinegar and oil into an enamel saucepan and place over a low heat.	Peel the baby corn and pick all of the 'silk' away from it.
Add the onions and carrots to the marinade, cover and stir well.	Count out 12 peppercorns and add them to the marinade.
Wash and 'top and tail' the baby French beans.	Wash and 'top and tail' the baby peas.
When the marinade has simmered with the onions and carrots for 10 minutes, add the corn, beans and peas. Cover and remove from the heat.	

Allow the marinade to cool for at least 30 minutes longer before serving in salad bowls. This salad may be kept in the refrigerator, covered, for 3–4 days.

HARVEST SALAD

You might think that salad is strictly a summer fare, consisting of the usual lettuce, tomato and cucumber. In fact, some of the best-tasting and nutritious salads can be made long after the traditional 'salad season' has departed. This salad has a beautiful autumn glow to its colouring and is plentiful in textures, vitamins, minerals and flavours. You could add other seasonal root vegetables or fruit that take your fancy. It takes 30 minutes to prepare and serves 2 adults and 2 children.

1 small turnip	2 red eating apples
1 medium onion	4 large leaves of white cabbage
2 large carrots	115g (4oz) of walnut halves
1 large beetroot	

Peel the turnip and onion. Grate them both finely into a large salad bowl.	Scrub the carrots and beetroot. Wash the apples.
Grate the carrots and the beetroot into the salad bowl.	Wash the cabbage leaves.
Quarter and core the apples and slice them into thin strips.	Pick out any debris from the walnut halves.
Shred one cabbage leaf into each of four serving bowls.	Add the apple and walnuts to the salad mixture. Stir well.

Spoon the salad over the cabbage leaf and serve immediately with your favourite dressing (try Smokey Bear Dressing, page 98).

SPOTTY SPUDS SALAD

A 'spud' was originally used to describe a spade or sharp tool used for gardening and farming. Of course, one of these would have been used to dig out potatoes from the ground. So the name stuck and potatoes are often called 'spuds'. These are spotted with parsley and garlic and may be served hot or cold. This recipe serves 2 adults and 2 children. It will take you 40 minutes, including the cooking time. Did you know that parsley eaten fresh should help prevent the odour of garlic from lingering on your breath?

900g (2lb) of new potatoes A bunch of fresh parsley 455g (1lb) of 'beef' tomatoes 3 cloves garlic	15ml (1 tablespoon) of cider vinegar 5ml (1 teaspoon) of dry mustard 30ml (2 tablespoons) of olive oil

Scrub the potatoes and steam them for 20 minutes or until they are tender.

Wash the parsley and shake or spin dry.

Wash the tomatoes and slice them into thin segments. Place them in the serving bowl.

Chop the parsley quite finely into the serving bowl. (You may use the stalks in a soup.)

Peel and crush the garlic into the serving bowl.

Measure the vinegar, mustard and olive oil into the bowl and stir well.

When the potatoes have cooked add them to the serving bowl. Stir the whole salad very well but gently.

Serve immediately or allow to cool and then chill for an hour.

3. RICE AND PASTA DISHES

JUMP AND SHOUT!

A crazy pasta dish so full of colour and texture that it looks ready to jump out of the dish! May be served hot or cold, taking about 30 minutes to prepare – including cooking time. Serves 2 adults and 2 children.

225g (8oz) of wholewheat pasta twists (fusilli) 2 stalks of celery 1 large carrot 1 medium onion	15g (½oz) fresh mint (or 10ml (2 teaspoons) dried) 15ml (1 tablespoon) of soya oil 285g (10oz) of sweetcorn 225g (8oz) of natural yogurt

Measure the pasta into a pan and cover with water. Bring to a slow boil then simmer until just tender to bite (about 12 minutes).

Scrub the celery and the carrot.

Chop the onion quite finely. Wash and chop the mint.

Slice the celery and the carrot into 2.5cm (1 inch) thin strips.

Heat the oil in a pan. Add the onion, celery, sweetcorn and carrot. Sauté them gently for 5–7 minutes.

Place the chopped mint in a jug with the yogurt and stir well.

Remove the vegetables from the heat and stir the yogurt mixture in with them. Do this gently so that the celery and carrot do not break up.

Drain the cooked pasta and pour it into the serving dish.

Stir the yogurt and vegetable mixture in with the pasta and serve immediately.

TOMATO TIZZY

'Tizzy' used to be slang for 'a sixpence' but now means something in a state of excitement – exactly like the tangle of spaghetti, garlic and onion in this dish. Allow 40 minutes to prepare, including the cooking. This serves 2 adults and 2 children. Idea: run through the alphabet calling out words that rhyme with tizzy, i.e. busy, dizzy, fizzy ...

2 litres (4 pints) of boiling water	15ml (3 teaspoons) of fresh basil (or 7.5ml (1½ teaspoons) of dried basil)
15ml (1 tablespoon) of soya oil	2 small onions
225g (8oz) of wholewheat spaghetti	4 whole fresh tomatoes
425g (15oz) of chopped tomato	Freshly ground black pepper
140g (5oz) of tomato paste	2 cloves of garlic

Boil the water in a large saucepan. Add the oil.	Measure out the spaghetti.
	Add the spaghetti to the water and stir it with a fork as it softens. Reduce the heat.
Pour the chopped tomato and the tomato paste into a small saucepan.	Wash and chop the basil (or just measure the dried basil).
Simmer the tomato mix for 5 minutes.	Stir the spaghetti again.
	Add the basil to the tomato mixture and stir well. Continue to let it simmer gently.
Peel the onions and slice them very finely. Separate each slice into rings and place them on one side.	
	Wash the fresh tomatoes and slice them into quarters or halves. Put to one side.

When the spaghetti has cooked until just tender, drain the liquid from it. Now add the onion rings to the spaghetti and toss them gently together using two large spoons.

Serve the spaghetti and onion onto four plates using a fork and a spoon.

Ladle some of the tomato sauce over the spaghetti and onion.

Sprinkle some freshly ground pepper over the sauce and place the fresh tomato pieces onto the centre of each serving.

Crush the garlic onto each serving, a little on each fresh tomato slice.

Serve immediately with a green salad side dish.

RAINBOW RICE

This multi-coloured, layered rice mould is made with Basmati rice to keep the colours soft and contrasting. Basmati can be purchased unpolished and organically grown, it simply has a lighter colour than brown rice. Serve this chilled then tipped out on a platter with a sauce or a salad garnish. It will take 45 minutes to prepare, including cooking time for the rice, but allow more time for it to chill. There is enough to serve 2 adults and 2 children.

455g (1lb) of Basmati rice 1 litre (approx. 2 pints) of cold water 4 fresh tomatoes 1 small green pepper 2 large eggs	60ml (4 tablespoons) of milk (soya or cow's) A little margarine 5ml (1 teaspoon) of paprika A soufflé dish or deep cake tin

	Pour the rice into a fine sieve and rinse under cold water.
Place the rice in a large saucepan with the water. Place over a medium heat and bring to the boil, stirring as necessary.	
	Wash the tomatoes and pepper. Remove the stalks and cores.
Reduce the rice to a slow simmer, stir and then cover.	
Cut the pepper into quarters along its length.	Take the quarters of pepper and slice them thinly along their length. Place them to one side.
Slice the tomatoes into thin rings. Place them to one side.	Crack two large eggs into a small jug or bowl. Add 60ml (4 tablespoons) of milk and whisk with a fork until it froths.
Pour the egg mixture into a small saucepan and cook over a gentle heat, whisking all the while with a fork. Do not overcook.	Use a little margarine to grease the soufflé dish or cake tin.

When the rice has absorbed all of the water, stir it well and begin to prepare the layers: spoon rice into the dish, pressing down as you add it, to the depth of 2.5cm (1 inch).

 Place half the green pepper slices on the pressed rice, spreading them evenly. Sprinkle a tiny bit of the paprika over the layer of pepper.

Add more rice.

 Place half of the tomato slices on the pressed rice, spreading them evenly. Sprinkle a tiny bit of the paprika over the layer of tomato.

Add more rice.

Now add all of the cooked egg, spread it and sprinkle with a tiny pinch of paprika.

Add more rice.

Repeat the layering process in reverse order: tomatoes, paprika, rice, peppers, paprika and rice. Press the rice down after each addition. Finally sprinkle a little paprika over the top of the pressed rice.

Place the completed dish in the fridge to chill. To serve, place a plate over the dish and invert. Allow it a minute or two to come away from the dish, then remove the dish and serve the rice mould with a salad or sauce.

STARS IN A BLIZZARD

This dish has a very delicate flavour and is easy to digest. The uncoloured rice is our blizzard, the turmeric-coloured rice grains are distant stars, and the lemon quarters are near stars. Speaking of which, do you know the names and distances from Earth of the two nearest stars? (Answer at the bottom of the page.) Only 30 minutes to make, including the cooking. Enough for 2 adults and 2 children.

340g (12oz) of Basmati rice 5ml (1 teaspoon) turmeric 1 lemon	115g (4oz) mixed ground nuts Pieces of bay-leaf 2.5ml ($\frac{1}{2}$ teaspoon) paprika

Wash the rice and divide it into two portions. Place them in separate pans and cover each with 340ml (12oz) of water, bring to the boil. Sprinkle 5ml (1 teaspoon) of turmeric into one portion as it cooks. Stir well.

Leave the rind on the lemon. Wash, slice one half into thin circles and remove the pips. Now cut each slice into four.

Drain the rice and squeeze the juice from the other lemon half over the coloured portion of rice.

Stir the ground nuts into the uncoloured portion of rice. Add the pieces of bay-leaf.

Mix the rice portions together in the serving dish and decorate with the lemon pieces. Now sprinkle the paprika over the top and serve.

Answer: the Sun is our closest star, being 92.9 million miles away. The next closest star is Alpha Proxima, which is 24,696,000 million miles away – 4.2 light years.

OODLES OF NOODLES

How do you eat noodles? Do you cut them up, or use a spoon, or do you try the old 'wrap it round a fork' trick? No one seems to have discovered a tidy way of eating them – some people even resort to putting one end in their mouth and sucking until the other end joins it! This is *extremely* messy because the noodle whips about leaving sauce all over faces, clothes and innocent bystanders. Perhaps you could invent a machine that tames wild noodles and lets you eat them safely? You could do a drawing of it during the 40 minutes this dish takes to cook. It will serve 2 adults and 2 children.

1 litre (approx. 2 pints)of water 225g (8oz) of wholewheat tagliatelle noodles 15ml (1 tablespoon) of cider vinegar 15ml (1 tablespoon) of brewer's yeast	15ml (1 tablespoon) of tamari 30g (1oz) of fresh parsley 30g (1oz) chopped Chives (or spring onion) 4 stalks of celery 225g (8oz) of firm tofu

Boil the water in a large pan.	Measure out the tagliatelle.
Add the noodles to the water and stir them well, then reduce them to a simmer.	
Measure the vinegar, yeast and tamari into a small saucepan and place over a low heat.	Wash the parsley, chives and celery and slice them all very thinly. Place them to one side.
Stir the noodles again.	Cut the tofu into small chunks. Place aside.
When the noodles are cooked to 'just tender', drain them and pour them immediately into a large ceramic bowl.	
	Add the parsley, chives, celery and tofu chunks to the noodles in the bowl. Use two large spoons to mix all together very well but gently.

Serve the noodle mixture into bowls and ladle some of the sauce over each portion. You may cover any remaining noodles and keep them warm in the oven. Try eating this dish with chopsticks.

TROPICAL RICE

This rice dish is perfect for days when it gets so hot that you don't feel like eating much, or for cold days when you dream of sun-kissed beaches. The tropics are the warm regions between two imaginary circles drawn above and below the Equator. (Do you know what they're called? Try checking in an atlas.) This takes 40 minutes to prepare and serves 2 adults and 2 children.

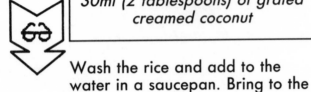

> 455g (1lb) of brown rice
> 1 litre (approx. 2 pints) of water
> 1 peach
> 1 orange
> 30ml (2 tablespoons) of grated creamed coconut
>
> 55g (2oz) of pine nuts
> 2 bay-leaves
> 5ml (1 teaspoon) of paprika (or chilli)

Wash the rice and add to the water in a saucepan. Bring to the boil.

Wash the peach and peel the orange.

Slice the peach in half and remove the stone. Now slice each half into thin strips. Put to one side.

Separate the orange into segments and pick off all of the pulp. Put to one side.

Stir the rice once again and reduce the heat somewhat.

Grate the creamed coconut and put to one side.

Heat the coconut, orange, peach and pine nuts in a pan over a low heat. Stir often to prevent sticking.

Wash the bay-leaves and break them into small pieces.

When the rice has absorbed all of the water drain it and pour it into a serving dish.

Add the cooked orange and peach segments, the grated coconut, the pine nuts and the bay-leaf pieces to the rice. Stir them together. Now sprinkle the paprika or chilli over all and serve.

Answer: (Tropics of Cancer & Capricorn).

44

BREAKFAST RICE

What! Eat rice for breakfast! That's right, lots of people, from all over the world, eat rice for breakfast, in fact *2 billion people* (2,000,000,000 people*) depend on rice for their basic food. In Japan, for instance, breakfast rice is called *asa gohan* (which literally means morning rice) and is served with tea and miso-soup. In parts of India and China, rice is mixed with spices and served as a background to sauces, nuts or cheese. Rice was brought to Spain in the eighth century, has travelled all of Europe (and the world) and is now grown in many countries. Rice may be eaten with chopsticks, fingers, folded bread, a fork or a spoon – depending on which country you are having breakfast in. This will serve 2 hungry children and takes 25 minutes to prepare.

*This is an American billion – a British billion is a thousand times bigger than an American one – 2,000,000,000,000.

225g (8oz) of brown rice *570ml (1 pint) of water* *2 large eggs*	*285ml ($\frac{1}{2}$ pint) of milk* *(soya or cow's)* *2.5ml ($\frac{1}{2}$ teaspoon) of* *ground nutmeg*

Wash the rice. Put it into a saucepan with the water. Bring to the boil.	Break the eggs into a small bowl and whisk them with a fork until they froth.
Reduce the rice to a simmer and stir once before covering.	Prepare two large breakfast bowls.
When the rice has absorbed all of the water, add the whisked egg and stir it into the rice. Keep the heat low and the stirring constant.	
Warm the milk.	Add the nutmeg to the rice mixture and continue stirring.

When the egg is completely cooked by the hot rice, spoon portions into the breakfast bowls and pour warm milk over each serving. Eat immediately.

PARSLEY MAZE

This is made with rice *and* pasta to create a textured dish with sparkles of green. It is most attractive served in individual baking dishes and then tipped out onto the plate. Allow an hour to prepare enough for 4 children (that includes the cooking.) Serve it hot or cold. Idea: while it's baking, draw a maze around a piece of string (or spaghetti) then remove the string and see if one of your friends can get through it.

2 litres (approx. 4 pints) of water 170g (6oz) of brown rice 170g (6oz) of wholewheat spaghetti 285ml (½ pint) of milk (soya or cow's)	2 eggs 15g (½oz) of fresh parsley 5ml (1 teaspoon) of dried thyme 170g (6oz) Cheddar cheese A little soya oil

Bring the water to the boil and divide between two saucepans.	Measure out the rice and spaghetti.
Simmer the rice in one pan, the spaghetti in the other until they are nearly tender, about 20 minutes.	Mix the milk and eggs in a jug. Whisk to a froth. Wash and chop the parsley.
Drain the liquid from the rice and spaghetti and pour them together into a large bowl.	Put the parsley and thyme in to the bowl.
Warm the oven to 180°C/350°F (Gas Mark 4).	Grate the cheese and add it to the rice, pasta and herbs.
Mix all the ingredients together using two large spoons.	Lightly oil the baking dishes.
Press the mixture firmly and evenly into each baking dish.	
	Pour the milk and egg mixture over the top of each serving.

Bake for 20–25 minutes at 180°C/350°F (Gas Mark 4). Serve hot with vegetables and a sauce; or serve cold with a side salad.

4. FLANS AND BAKES

FLAKEY FLAN PASTRY

It used to be frightening to eat pastry made from wholewheat flour. Table items needed to be arranged around one's plate to ensure that the pastry ricocheted inwards and not onto someone else's skull. Even the old joke about cardboard did not apply – more like steel plate! I promise that this is different. It takes 10 minutes to prepare and makes enough for two 20cm (8 inch) or one 37.5cm (15 inch) flan cases.

140ml ($\frac{1}{4}$ pint) of water	55g (2oz) of wholewheat
340g ($\frac{3}{4}$lb) of wholewheat flour	'sprinkling' flour
115g (4oz) of margarine or butter	A rolling pin

Bring the water to the boil. Allow it to cool slightly.

Measure the flour into a large mixing bowl.

Measure the margarine or butter into the bowl and begin to work it into the flour with a fork.

Now add the hot water to the flour mix. Stir with a fork then knead the mix with your hand.

Leave the mixture while a flan filling is prepared.

Flour a board and rolling pin with the 'sprinkling' flour. Knead the pastry once again and shape it into a round ball.

Roll the pastry into a thin round. Roll it onto the rolling pin and lift it over the flan case. Centre it and slowly unroll it. Now press it into the flan case corners, trim or flute the edges and fill the casing with the mixture you have prepared.

SLUGS AND SNAILS

Both of these creatures are *gastropod molluscs*, one lives entirely on land, the other on both land and water. Do you know which lives entirely on land? This flan is sweet and savoury with 'slugs' and 'snails' sleeping on top. You will need 45 minutes to prepare it and 30 minutes cooking time. This serves 2 adults and 2 children. Note: *real* slugs and snails do *not* like sleeping on flans.

One mixture of the Flakey Flan Pastry recipe (see page 47) 225g (8oz) of dried figs 2 medium onions 1 large potato	115g (4oz) of button mushrooms 2 eggs 200ml ($\frac{1}{3}$ pint) of milk (soya or cow's) A food processor

Prepare the pastry mix (page 47) and press it into a large flan dish.	Wash the figs in a bowl of warm water. Remove any pieces of stem.
Warm the oven to 180°C/350°F (Gas Mark 4). Peel the onions and scrub the potato. Chop both finely in the food processor.	Slice 6 figs as finely as you can and put them to one side.
Clean and trim the mushrooms and slice them into halves. Put to one side with the sliced figs.	Put the eggs and milk in the processor. Purée with the remaining figs.
Stir the chopped onions and potato in with the purée of egg, milk and figs. Pour the mixture into the flan case.	
	Arrange the mushroom halves (they are the snails) and the fig slices (they are the slugs) onto the top of the flan.

Bake it for 30 minutes at 180°C/350°F (Gas Mark 4). Serve hot with a salad.

Answer: the slug lives entirely on land.

BEE IN A BONNET

These little pastry bonnets have a tangy 'bee' of garlic in the middle. They take 45 minutes to prepare and 25–30 minutes to cook. Eight bonnets are ample fare for 2 adults and 2 children. Serve them hot with vegetables or a salad, or chill them overnight and have them in your lunch-box.

One mixture of the Flakey Flan Pastry recipe (page 47) 8 cloves of garlic 15g (½oz) fresh parsley	1 large onion 455g (1lb) of potatoes 225g (½lb) of fresh peas 15ml (1 tablespoon) of soya oil

Make up the Flakey Flan Pastry recipe. Warm the oven to 180°C/350°F (Gas Mark 4).

Peel the garlic cloves and wash the parsley.

Finely chop or slice the onion.

Scrub the potatoes and weigh the peas.

Dice the potatoes and sauté them with the onions in the oil for 5–7 minutes. Add the fresh peas, stir well and remove the sauté from the heat. Cover.

Chop the parsley quite finely.

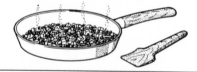

Roll out the pastry.

Cut eight 10cm (4 inch) circles or squares from the pastry.

Place a spoonful of the vegetable mixture in the centre of each pastry.

Press one garlic clove into the vegetable filling in each pastry. Sprinkle some chopped parsley over each clove.

Fold the pastry up over the filling and pinch the edges together.

Pinch the edges more firmly together to make a fancy 'frill' along the top of the 'bonnet'.

Bake the bonnets at 180°C/350°F (Gas Mark 4) for 25–30 minutes or until they are a lovely golden brown on top.

BUNDLES OF STICKS

These are little bread bundles full of vegetable sticks. The idea comes from reading stories about country children of long ago who had to collect bundles of sticks for their home fires. Bundles of sticks have always had a special significance in history (here are three for you to investigate: Good King Wenceslas, Fascism, and the I Ching). There's also an ancient game you can play: grasp 49 orange-sticks or straws together and stand them in a bundle on a table. Now release them quickly so that they fall in a heap. Each player takes another stick and trys to flip one stick at a time from the heap on the table. No stick other than the one being lifted must move – if it does it is the other player's turn. The player who takes the most sticks from the pile wins. This dish takes 30 minutes to prepare and 30 minutes to cook. There is enough here for 2 adults and 2 children.

1 large potato 2 large carrots 2 large parsnips 16 spring onions * 455g (1lb) of wholewheat flour	15ml (3 teaspoons) of baking powder 55g (2oz) of margarine or butter 285ml (10fl oz) of water (approx.) A rolling pin

	Scrub the potato, carrots and parsnips.
Slice the vegetables into long strips: approximately eight from each of the parsnips and carrots, the potato into chip-size strips.	Wash and trim the spring onions and slice them in half along their length.
	In a large bowl, mix the flour and baking powder.
Rub the butter or margarine into the flour mixture until the texture is quite even.	Measure the water into a jug.
	Add the water to the flour and stir with a fork first, then use your hands to work the dough.

Sprinkle some flour on a board and on a rolling pin. Place the dough onto the board and roll it out to 1cm ($\frac{3}{8}$ inch) thickness. Now slice the dough into strips about 2.5cm (1 inch) wide and 10cm (8 inches) long. Lift them gently from the board and place them to one side.

Warm the oven to 190°C/375°F (Gas Mark 5).

Begin to make the bundles: take a strip of dough and lie it flat. Now take a selection of potato, carrot, parsnip and spring onion slices. Place these in the centre of each strip of dough, (across its length). Wrap the dough round the sticks once.

As each bundle gets handed to you, continue to wrap the bread dough around the sticks in a spiral towards each end. Pinch the dough onto itself and place the completed bundle onto a lightly oiled baking tray.

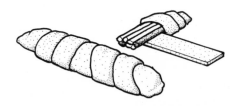

Repeat this procedure until all of the bundles are on the tray. Bake them for 30 minutes at 190°C/375°F (Gas Mark 5). Serve immediately with a vegetable gravy or allow to cool and use for lunch-box or snacks.

FLORIDA FLAN

I once visited an aunt and uncle in Florida who weren't convinced that a person could live without you-know-what. I cooked their whole family a meatless meal just to show what *they* were missing. This was one dish in the main course (the next recipe was also included). I prepared that meal for ten people — this will serve 2 adults and 2 children. Allow 1½ hours for the complete preparation (that includes making the pastry and the cooking time).

One Flakey Flan Pastry recipe mix (page 47) 455g (1lb) of fresh spinach 1 large onion	A little soya oil 455g (1lb) of Cheddar cheese Freshly ground black pepper

Prepare the pastry mix and line a deep flan case with it.	Wash the spinach and trim the centre stalks from it.
Peel and slice the onion. Sauté it in a little soya oil. Warm the oven to 180°C/350°F (Gas Mark 4).	Slice the spinach into 1cm ($\frac{3}{8}$ inch) strips and drain them in a colander.
Grate the cheese.	Spread a thin layer of sautéed onion in the flan case.
Grind some black pepper over the onion.	
	Spread some sliced spinach over the onion, pressing down as you do so.
Now sprinkle 115g (4oz) of the grated cheese over the spinach, add some more ground pepper.	
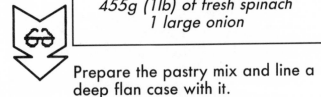	Spread another layer of sautéed onion over the grated cheese. Spread more spinach over the onion, pressing it down also.
Sprinkle another 115g (4oz) of grated cheese over the spinach. Now add some more ground pepper.	

Spread the remaining sautéed onion over the cheese. Add the rest of the sliced spinach and press down firmly. (Please note: the spinach may actually rise above the level of the flan case without causing problems.)

Grind some black pepper over the spinach and top the flan with all the remaining grated Cheddar.

The flan should bake for a total of 30–40 minutes or until the pastry is golden brown and the spinach quite tender. Serve immediately or allow it to cool and serve cold with a salad.

PEPPER PROTEST

This was served up with the Florida Flan. A great bag full of red and green peppers brought cries of protest: no one supposed that anything much could be made of them. This dish turned protest into praise. Choose colourful peppers, only 'just ripe' and about 10–12.5cm (4–5 inches) long. This will make enough for 2 adults and 2 children. Allow 45 minutes for preparation and cooking.

4 peppers (red, green or yellow) 115g (4oz) of fresh parsley 455g (1lb) of button mushrooms	30ml (2 tablespoons) of cooking wine 2 small onions Some aluminium foil

Slice the peppers in half along their length. Remove the pulp and the stalks.

Wash the parsley and remove the coarse stems. Chop the leaves quite finely and place them to one side.

Wash the mushrooms.

Wash the halved peppers.

Leave a dozen mushrooms whole. Slice the rest and spread a layer of them into a shallow casserole dish. Pour the cooking wine over the sliced mushrooms.

Fill each pepper half with some chopped parsley. Use up all of the parsley between the eight pepper halves — about 15g ($\frac{1}{2}$oz) per pepper half.

Peel and slice the onions. Warm the oven to 180°C/350°F (Gas Mark 4).

Place some sliced onion over each parsley-filled pepper half.

Arrange the filled peppers in the casserole dish. Place a whole mushroom at intervals between them.

Cover the casserole with the tin foil and bake for 20 minutes at 180°C/350°F (Gas Mark 4). Remove the foil and serve immediately, spooning the sauce and mushrooms over all.

NINE-TO-FIVE STEW

This is a rich, wintery stew so thick you can stand a spoon up in it. Aim to make the preparation time as brief as possible – before work or school. But let this cook for as long as possible — from nine to five will do – at a very low cooking temperature. Enough here for 4 hungry adults and 4 very hungry children. Be sure to use quite a large stew-pot with a lid. And don't peek before it's ready.

455g (1lb) of swedes	10ml (2 teaspoons) of whole cloves
455g (1lb) of carrots	
455g (1lb) of parsnips	455g (16oz) of chestnut purée
455g (1lb) of turnips	2 litres (approx. 4 pints) of water
900g (2lb) of potatoes	
455g (1lb) of small onions	12 whole peppercorns

Wash the swedes and peel them.

Scrub the carrots, parsnips, turnips, and potatoes.

Slice the parsnips and carrots in half along their length and then cut them into 2.5cm (1 inch) chunks.

Slice the turnips and swedes into 2.5cm (1 inch) chunks.

Peel the onions and place to one side.

Slice the potatoes into 2.5cm (1 inch) chunks.

Place the chopped vegetables in a very large enamel or cast-iron stew-pot and stir them together.

Select whole cloves from your supply and push one into each end of each small onion.

Stir the chestnut purée into 2 litres (4 pints) of water.

Add 12 whole peppercorns to the vegetables in the stew-pot.

Pour the chestnut stock over the vegetables and stir the whole mixture very well.

Add the onions pierced with whole cloves to the vegetable mix. Stir the stew again, very gently.

Cover the pot and place the stew in the oven at a very low temperature – 140°C/275°F (Gas Mark 1) will do nicely. Leave it to serve the stew. Serve this in big, colourful bowls with lots of wholewheat bread.

PIZZA ALRIGHT!

Whenever you feel like saying: 'For pizza-ache! Give me some pizza quiet!', you should try making this pizza. It's so easy, it's a real pizza cake! This recipe reveals some of my time-tested secrets (I'm giving you a pizza my mind), and will make two 30cm (12 inch) pizzas. For this pizza the action you will need one hour for preparation and 40 minutes to cook. Do you know a six-letter word that means the same as the letter 'z'? (Clue – it's somewhere in this book.) Now spell 'pizza' using the new six-letter word. (Answer at the end of the recipe.)

425ml (¾ pint) of water
15ml (1 tablespoon) of
dried yeast
5ml (1 teaspoon) of
raw cane sugar
455g (1lb) of
wholewheat flour
*
1 green pepper
225g (½lb) of button mushrooms
2 onions

140g (5oz) of tomato paste
570ml (1 pint) of water
5ml (1 teaspoon) of basil
5ml (1 teaspoon) of oregano
Garlic to taste
340g (12oz) of Cheddar
(or Mozzarella) cheese
30ml (2 tablespoons) of soya oil
Freshly ground black pepper
to taste
A rolling pin

Boil 425ml (¾ pint) of water and allow it to cool to blood temperature.

Measure the dried yeast and raw cane sugar into a jug.

Pour the warm water over the yeast and sugar. Stir well to prevent any lumps forming. Allow the yeast to work for 10 minutes.

Measure the flour into a large bowl.

Stir the yeast into the flour using a fork first, then a spoon. Add more water if necessary to bring the dough to a 'kneadable' consistency. Now cover the dough with a cloth and leave it on one side to rise for 15 minutes.

Wash the green pepper and the button mushrooms.

Peel and chop two onions.

Slice the mushrooms in half.

Remove the stem and pulp from the green pepper and slice it into thin strips along its length.

56

Mix the tomato paste and 570ml (1 pint) of water together in a jug. Add the dried basil and oregano to the sauce. Add crushed garlic to taste. Stir.

Grate the Cheddar (or Mozzarella) cheese onto a plate.

The dough may now be kneaded gently and divided into two parts.

Arrange all of the prepared vegetables, the sauce and the cheese in a half circle on the table — a sort of assembly line.

Lightly flour a board and roll the portions of dough into thin circles.

Pour the oil between the baking trays you will be using. Spread it out with your hands to cover the whole tray.

Warm the oven to 180°C/350°F (Gas Mark 4).

Press the pizza bases onto the oiled baking trays and allow them to rise for 20 minutes.

Bake the pizza bases for 10 minutes.

Spread the onions onto the partly baked bases.

Arrange the sliced mushrooms over the onions.

Arrange the sliced green pepper over the mushrooms.

Sprinkle ground pepper over the vegetables to suit your taste.

Spoon the tomato sauce over the vegetables, spreading it right to the edges of the pizzas.

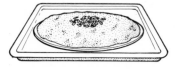

Sprinkle a thin layer of cheese over each of the pizzas, using only half of the 340g (12oz) at this point.

Bake the pizzas for 30 minutes at 180°C/350°F (Gas Mark 4). Remove them from the oven and sprinkle the remaining grated cheese over them. Turn the oven heat off and return the pizzas to the oven while you prepare the plates and call everyone to the table. Slice and serve immediately.

Answer: PIIZZARDIZZARDA P-I-IZZARD-IZZARD-A

ROBBERS OF THE LAST SPOON

When archaeologists dig out the ruins of lost civilizations, they have to draw each pebble, each change of soil colour or texture, and every other item visible in the walls of their excavations. From that information they can tell how people lived hundreds or thousands of years ago. The subtle earth-colours of this dish and the variety in its texture show up best if you bake it in a glass dish. This makes enough for 2 adults and 2 children. You will need 20 minutes preparation time and 45 minutes cooking time.

1 very large swede *115g (4oz) of raisins* *1 large onion* *2 cooking apples* *55g (2oz) of fresh, wholewheat breadcrumbs*	*Freshly ground black pepper* *10ml (2 teaspoons) of ground allspice* *55g (2oz) of Cheddar cheese*

Wash and peel the swede and cut it into 2.5cm (1 inch) chunks. Put aside.	Rinse the raisins and pick out any stems. Put aside.
Peel and thinly slice the onion and put the slices to one side.	Wash the cooking apples.
Quarter and core the apples and slice them thinly along their length. Warm the oven to 190°C/375°F (Gas mark 5).	Measure out the breadcrumbs and sprinkle them with freshly ground black pepper.
Measure out the ground allspice.	Begin to place the ingredients into the baking dish: a layer each of swede, raisins, onions, apples and a pinch of allspice.
Grate the cheese and put to one side.	Repeat the layers until all of the ingredients are used up.
Sprinkle the grated cheese over the top of the dish.	
	Cover the cheese with the fresh breadcrumbs and ground pepper mix.

Place the dish in the oven for 45 minutes at 190°C/375°F (Gas Mark 5). The swedes should be tender if pierced through with a fork or sharp knife. Serve hot with dark green, leafy vegetables.

FLECK AND CHECKER FLAN

Flecks are flakes of colour and this flan has plenty of them, thanks to the variety of vegetables included in it. The 'checker' is the lattice of pastry on top. Serve this hot or cold, but always with other colourful foods. There is enough here for 2 adults and 4 children. You will need 45 minutes to prepare and 45 minutes to cook. Appoint a Chancellor of the Fleck & Checker to slice and serve the flan.

1 Flakey Flan Pastry mix (page 47) 1 large turnip 2 carrots 2 onions 1 green pepper 1 red pepper	225g (8oz) of Cheddar cheese 55g (2oz) of Parmesan cheese 10ml (2 teaspoons) of freshly ground black pepper 2 eggs 30ml (2 tablespoons) of milk (soya or cow's)

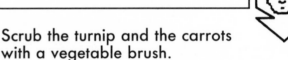

Prepare the pastry mix. Warm the oven to 180°C/350°F (Gas Mark 4).	Scrub the turnip and the carrots with a vegetable brush.
Peel and finely chop the onions. Place to one side.	Wash both peppers and slice them in half. Remove the pulp.
Grate the turnip and carrots and place them to one side.	Carefully slice the peppers into thin pieces. Put to one side.
	Grate the Cheddar.
Measure the Parmesan into a small bowl and stir in the pepper.	Mix the eggs and milk in a jug. Use a fork and bring them to a froth.
Roll some pastry out into a circle and press into a flan case. Roll the remaining pastry into a rectangle and cut it into 1cm ($\frac{3}{8}$ inch) strips.	Mix all of the vegetables and grated cheese together in a large bowl so that the mix is of even consistency.

Begin to weave the strips of pastry into a lattice pattern. You may wish to share this job, or you may wish to fight for the pleasure! It is very satisfying. Make the lattice larger than you think necessary, then leave it on the worktop when you have finished.

Spread the vegetable mixture into the flan case and press it down.

Slowly pour the egg and milk mixture over the vegetables.

Sprinkle the Parmesan and pepper mixture over the top of the flan.

Gently lift the lattice of pastry onto the flan. Press the edges together and trim any surplus. Bake for 45 minutes at 180°C/350°F (Gas Mark 4). Serve hot or cold.

POTATO ALLIUM

Allium is a family of plants made up of onions, garlic, leeks, chives etc. If you find one member of the family offensive, there is sure to be another you find pleasing. In this dish, the potato is alternated with the allium (whichever you select). There is enough here for 2 adults and 2 children. You will need 20 minutes preparation time, and 40 minutes for cooking. By the way: do you know which plant family the potato belongs to? (Answer at the end of the recipe.)

> 900g (2lb) of potatoes
> 4 cloves of garlic
> (or 2 medium onions or
> 2 large leeks or 60ml
> (4 tablespoons) of chives)
> 10ml (2 teaspoons) of
> dry mustard
>
> 15ml (1 tablespoon)of
> wholewheat flour
> 570ml (1 pint) of milk
> (soya or cow's)
> 15ml (1 tablespoon) of
> margarine or butter
> Freshly ground black pepper
> 4 cream crackers

Warm the oven to 180°C/350°F (Gas Mark 4).

Scrub the potatoes. Cut each one in half.

Peel and thinly slice the garlic, onion, leeks or chives.

Mix the mustard with the wholewheat flour.

Slice the potato halves into circles. Put them to one side.

Measure the milk into a jug.

Measure the margarine or butter into a small saucepan. Melt the butter then sprinkle the flour and mustard mixture onto it. Stir constantly as it thickens.

Pour small amounts of the milk into the saucepan and stir. The mixture will thicken. Use all of the milk, a little at a time.

Spread a layer of sliced potato on the bottom of a casserole.

Spread a layer of 'allium' over the layer of potato slices.

62

Sprinkle some freshly ground
black pepper over the allium.

 Pour one quarter of the mustard
sauce over those three layers.

Repeat the layers of sliced potato, allium, ground pepper and
mustard sauce three times more. Take turns pouring the mustard
sauce.

Crumble four cream crackers over
the top layer of sauce.

Bake at 180°C/350°F (Gas Mark 4) for 40 minutes without a cover.
Serve hot.

Answer: the potato is a member of the Solanum family. So are the
tomato and aubergine (eggplant).

SQUASH RACKET

A squash plant is a relative of the marrow but has a deep orange colour with a stronger, earthy flavour. Other members of the family are the pumpkin and the gourd. 'Racket' describes the criss-cross of cuts into the squash, but it could describe the noise you'll make talking about the flavour of this bake. Serve hot with lots of other vegetables and a dollop of Loon Butter (page 101). Serves 2 adults and 2 children. Allow an hour in total.

A 900g (2lb) squash
15ml (1 tablespoon) of dried parsley
or 30g (1oz) fresh parsley
15ml (1 tablespoon) of dried mint

or 30g (1oz) of fresh mint
3 cloves garlic
1 small onion
Aluminium foil

Slice the squash in half along its length and scrape away the seed pulp. Now rinse it with water.

Measure out the parsley and mint and mix them together. If using fresh herbs, give them a wash and chop fine.

Peel the garlic and onion. Crush the garlic and finely chop the onion.

Tear two pieces of aluminium foil big enough to wrap around each of the squash halves.

Warm the oven to 180°C/350°F (Gas Mark 4).

Use a fork to mix the herbs together with the chopped onions and crushed garlic.

Cut a deep criss-cross pattern into the squash without cutting the skin.

Rub the herb and onion mixture well into the lattice work.

Wrap the tin foil around each half and place the squash on a tray in the oven. Bake at 180°C/350°F (Gas Mark 4) for 30 minutes. Remove the foil and bake for another 15 minutes to brown slightly. Serve immediately.

1. Beaver's Dam Soup (page 11).

2. Metamorphosis Soup (page 12).

3. Big Yawn Soup (page 13).

4. Dandelion at Noon (page 14).

5. Royal Decree Soup (page 16).

6. Vegetable Stock (page 17).

7. Summer Lakes Soup (page 18).

8. Genghis Khan Broth (page 19).

9. Pot Belly Soup (page 20).

10. ABC Soup (page 21).

11. Paul Bunyan's Tears (page 22).

12. Dragon's Tooth Soup (page 23).

13. Green Lace Fruit Salad (page 24).

14. Needles in a Haystack (page 25).

15. Faeries' Glen Salad (page 26).

16. Verdi Presto Salad (page 28).

17. Preservation Salad (page 29).

18. Capillary Action Salad (page 30).

19. Botanists' Salad (page 31).

20. Sunrise Salad (page 32).

21. Sailor's Marinade (page 34).

22. Harvest Salad (page 35).

23. Spotty Spuds Salad (page 36).

24. Jump and Shout! (page 37).

25. Tomato Tizzy (page 38).

26. Rainbow Rice (page 40).

27. Stars in a Blizzard (page 42).

28. Oodles of Noodles (page 43).

29. Tropical Rice (page 44).

30. Breakfast Rice (page 45).

31. Parsley Maze (page 46).

32. Flakey Flan Pastry (page 47).

33. Slugs and Snails (page 48).

34. Bee in a Bonnet (page 49).

35. Bundles of Sticks (page 50).

36. Florida Flan (page 52).

37. Pepper Protest (page 54).

38. Nine-to-Five Stew (page 55).

39. Pizza Alright! (page 56).

40. Robbers of the Last Spoon (page 58).

41. Fleck and Checker Flan (page 60).

42. Potato Allium (page 62).

43. Squash Racket (page 64).

44. Carob Crinkles (page 65).

45. Speedy Spot of Luck (page 66).

46. For-Goodness-Sake-Cake (page 68).

47. Rib Stickers (page 70).

48. Blackstrap Biscuits (page 71).

49. Re-Baked Bread (page 72).

50. Sherlock Holmes Cake (page 73).

51. Sweet Briar Bread (page 74).

52. Bear-Paw Cake (page 76).

53. Almost Pretzels (page 78).

54. Vampire Bread (page 80).

55. Walnut Winks (page 82).

56. Spicey Kisses (page 83).

57. Flappers! (page 84).

58. Seeds for the Sowers (page 86).

59. Flies in the Buttermilk (page 88).

60. Pipestone Porridge (page 89).

61. Eggs is Eggs (page 90).

62. Red and Ginger Duet (page 92).

63. Pullet Surprise (page 93).

64. The Bed Spread (page 94).

65. Mighty Mouth Dressing (page 95).

66. Better-Than-Gravy (page 96).

67. Turtle River Spread (page 97).

68. Smokey Bear Dressing (page 98).

69. Meltability Sauce (page 99).

70. White-Water Dip (page 100).

71. Loon Butter (page 101).

72. Barbara Cute Sauce (page 102).

73. Make in Haste Paste (page 103).

74. Bells of Whitechapel Sauce (page 104).

75. Hedghog on a Log (page 105).

76. Fruity Goop (page 106).

77. June Bugs (page 107).

78. Goober Berry Bowl (page 108).

79. Twiddles (page 109).

80. Tornado Chill (page 110).

81. Wading Birds Snack (page 111).

82. Voyageurs' Munch (page 112).

83. Fireflies and Glow-worms (page 113).

84. Banana Burgers (page 114).

85. Nuts and Bolts (page 115).

86. Citrus Pucker (page 116).

87. Apple Jolly (page 117).

88. Rhubarb Razzmatazz (page 118).

89. Short, Fat and Sassy (page 119).

90. Peach Fury (page 120).

91. Alligator Whip (page 121).

92. Herb Snuggles (page 122).

93. Liquorice Limerick (page 124).

94. Blackberry Bragg (page 125).

95. Banana Flake Shake (page 126).

96. Minnehaha Splash (page 127).

5. BREADS, CAKES AND BISCUITS

CAROB CRINKLES

These chewy, crinkly biscuits have the nearly-chocolate flavour of carob. There are enough here for four dozen Crinkles, as friends, children and other animals will appear from everywhere when they smell them baking. Just 20 minutes preparation time and 15 minutes to cook.

55g (2oz) of carob powder 115g (4oz) of rolled oats 225g (8oz) of wholewheat flour 115g (4oz) of raw cane sugar	10ml (2 teaspoons) of baking powder 115g (4oz) of margarine or butter 55g (2oz) of ground nuts 285ml (10fl oz) of milk (soya or cow's) or water

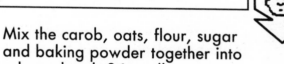

Warm the oven to 190°C/375°F (Gas Mark 5).

Mix the carob, oats, flour, sugar and baking powder together into a large bowl. Stir well.

Use a fork to work the margarine evenly into the dry mix.

Add the ground nuts to the mix. Stir well.

Gradually add the milk or water to the mix. Stir well.

Lightly oil a baking sheet.

Drop walnut-sized balls of dough onto the baking sheet.

Use a fork to press the balls of dough flat: press once in each direction to form a criss-cross, crinkle pattern.

Bake at 190°C/375°F (Gas Mark 5) for 15 minutes. Allow to cool on racks.

SPEEDY SPOT OF LUCK

I invented this quick and easy bread recipe by accident during a log-cabin holiday. Far from anywhere and running low on basic supplies, I thought there was nothing I could possibly make to fill the hollow in our stomachs. But luck smiled on me and I've been making this ever since. These two small loaves take 15 minutes to prepare, only 30 minutes to bake and will serve 4 adults. A savoury quick-bread that is delicious with soups, salad or cheese. Idea — if *you* were snowed-up in a log cabin, what ten items would you most like to find in your cupboard?

1 small onion
45ml (3 tablespoons) of soya oil
285g (10oz) of 81 per cent flour
10ml (2 teaspoons) of baking powder
285ml (10fl oz) of water

15ml (1 tablespoon) of herb blend
(try a mixture of dried thyme and parsley)
1 egg
A rolling pin

Chop the onion finely and sauté in 15ml (1 tablespoon) of the soya oil. Warm the oven to 190°C/375°F (Gas Mark 5).

Mix the flour and baking powder together in a bowl.

Measure the water and 30ml (2 tablespoons) of oil onto the flour mixture.

Use a large spoon to stir the water and oil into the dry mix.

Mix your selection of herbs together.

Sprinkle some flour on a board and use a floured rolling pin to roll the bread dough into a 1cm ($\frac{3}{8}$ inch) thick rectangle.

Spread the herb mixture evenly over the rectangle of dough.

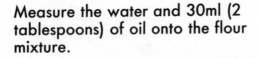

Roll the rectangle in on itself along its length. Pinch the edges together and slice the roll into halves.

Place the halves on a baking tray.

Stir the sautéed onions in with the egg and whisk.

66

Spread half of the egg and onion mixture onto each loaf.

 Bake at 190°C/375°F (Gas Mark 5) for 30 minutes. Allow them to cool then slice into thick pieces and serve.

THE FOR-GOODNESS-SAKE-CAKE

This is a sugar-less cake with a light, crumbly texture. It uses ingredients that should be readily available in every healthy kitchen. Another name for it could be the Demolition Cake because it gets demolished once it's put out. Allow 20 minutes to prepare it and 40 minutes cooking time. There is *usually* enough for 2 adults and 2 children.

115g (4oz) of wholewheat flour
115g (4oz) of rolled oats
55g (2oz) of wheat bran
115g (4oz) of raisins
2.5ml ($\frac{1}{2}$ teaspoon) of ground cinnamon

2.5ml ($\frac{1}{2}$ teaspoon) of ground cloves
5ml (1 teaspoon) of baking powder
285ml (10fl oz) of water or fruit juice
60ml (2fl oz) of soya oil

Set the oven to 180°C/350°F (Gas Mark 4).

Mix the flour, oats, bran, raisins, cinnamon, cloves and baking powder together in a large bowl. Use a fork to mix them very well so that there are no lumps or streaks.

Now measure the water or fruit juice into a jug and pour the oil over it.

Stir this liquid into the dry mixture in your bowl. Use a large spoon to make sure it is evenly mixed.

Oil a 20cm (8 inch) square baking tin.

Spoon the moist mixture into the tin and spread it evenly.

Pop the cake into the oven and let it cook for 40 minutes on the top shelf.

When you take it out it should be nicely brown. Let it cool before you slice into it. Serve it on its own or with a spoonful of honey over the top.

RIB STICKERS

As children, we often played in woods and overgrown land. That meant we came home covered in 'stickers', which are burs and prickly seeds that cling to clothing in the hope that they will be taken somewhere where they can propagate. These bread sticks cling to your ribs instead. They take only 50 minutes — including the cooking. This recipe makes enough for 2 adults and 2 children.

340g (12oz) of wholewheat flour 285ml ($\frac{1}{2}$ pint) of water 5ml (1 teaspoon) of dried thyme 5ml (1 teaspoon) of sea salt 15ml (1 tablespoon) of Parmesan	30ml (2 tablespoons) of soya oil 55g (2oz) of sesame seeds 30g (1oz) of poppy seeds 1 small onion A little soya oil

Measure the flour into a large mixing bowl.	Measure the water into a jug.
Add the thyme, salt and Parmesan to the flour. Stir well.	Measure the soya oil onto the water.
Pour the oil and water over the flour mix. Stir well with a wooden spoon.	Weigh out the sesame seeds and poppy seeds into a small bowl. Stir well.
Warm the oven to 180°C/350°F (Gas Mark 4).	
Peel and finely chop the onion.	Spread some oil on your hands.
	Begin to knead the dough to 'wake up' the gluten.
Add the onion to the dough.	Continue kneading.
	Divide the dough into small portions and roll them into long, thin sticks.
Roll the 'stickers' in the seed mixture. Use a firm pressure while rolling them to ensure that the seeds stick to the stickers!	Lightly oil the baking trays.
Place them on baking trays. Bake them for 25 minutes at 180°C/350°F (Gas Mark 4).	

BLACKSTRAP BISCUITS

Blackstrap is the dark molasses left after cane sugar has been through three stages of the boiling and crystallization process. It has minerals (iron and calcium) that give it some nutritional value and has a sharp, semi-sweet flavour. Sugar wasn't really known in Britain until the year 1299 and even for many years afterwards it was extremely expensive, and therefore only available in very small amounts. This makes 2½ dozen, enough for 2 adults and 4 children, and takes only 45 minutes to prepare, including the cooking time.

340g (12oz) of wholewheat flour 5ml (1 teaspoon) of ground cinnamon 2.5ml (½ teaspoon) of ground nutmeg 5ml (1 teaspoon) of baking powder	60ml (2fl oz) of soya oil 60ml (2fl oz) of hot water 55g (2oz) of honey 55g (2oz) of blackstrap molasses 1 egg

Measure the flour into a large mixing bowl.

Sprinkle the cinnamon and nutmeg into the flour mixture. Stir very well.	Add the baking powder to the dry mixture.
Pour the oil into a jug with the hot water.	Scoop the honey and molasses onto the flour mix.
Whisk the egg in with the oil and water in the jug.	Stir the dry mixture slowly but thoroughly with a large spoon.
Warm the oven to 180°C/350°F (Gas Mark 4).	Add the liquid from the jug to the dry mix and keep stirring.

Drop the dough onto baking trays with a teaspoon.

Bake them for 20 minutes at 180°C/350°F (Gas Mark 4). Allow them to cool on a rack and store them in an airtight container.

RE-BAKED BREAD

All of those ends of loaves and day-old slices can be put to very good use by jazzing them up with herbs and spices. Cut the bread into crouton-size cubes or be creative and use kitchen scissors to cut stars and moons and all variety of shapes. These take only 30 minutes to prepare and re-bake. Then float them in soups or stews, or eat them with spreads or dips. They will store in an air-tight container for up to one week.

30ml (2 tablespoons) of soya oil	5ml (1 teaspoon) of dried thyme
115g (4oz) of wholewheat bread	5ml (1 teaspoon) of paprika
10ml (2 teaspoons) of dried parsley	15ml (1 tablespoon) of celery seed
	Kitchen scissors

Pour the oil into a jar.

Begin to cut the bread into cubes, strips, or other shapes.

Add the parsley, thyme, paprika and celery seed to the oil. Shake well.

Warm the oven to 150°C/300°F (Gas Mark 2).

Pour the oil mixture onto a baking tray and spread it round.

Place the bread shapes on the tray and move them about to absorb some of the oil mixture.

Use a fork or spatula to turn the shapes over to absorb more of the oil mixture.

Bake the shapes at 150°C/300°F (Gas Mark 2) for 20 minutes, turning them once or twice to absorb all of the oil. Allow the shapes to become quite dry before removing them from the oven. Use these immediately or allow them to cool and store away in an airtight container.

SHERLOCK HOLMES CAKE

A slice of this cake *cannot* be stolen without leaving lots of crumbs as evidence. But if someone could ever manage to steal a whole one, Holmes would simply send Dr Watson to make certain it wasn't eaten all at once — the aroma is clue enough as to its whereabouts. How do we know that Sherlock Holmes loved cakes? (Answer at the bottom of the page.) Allow one hour to make this cake, including cooking time. This makes a 23cm×33cm (9 inch×13 inch) cake, enough for 4 adults and 4 children.

455g (1lb) of wholewheat flour	115g (4oz) of raw cane sugar
225g (8oz) of dried currants	60ml (4 tablespoons) of soya oil
115g (4oz) of rolled oats	2.5ml ($\frac{1}{2}$ teaspoon) of ground ginger
7.5ml ($1\frac{1}{2}$ teaspoons) of baking powder	570ml (1 pint) of fruit juice
	55g (2oz) of citrus peel
	55g (2oz) of almond flakes

	Weigh the flour into a large mixing bowl.
Measure the currants into another bowl.	Add the oats and baking powder to the flour.
Sprinkle the sugar over the currants. Pour the oil over the sugar. Stir well.	Measure the ground ginger into the dry mix. Stir well.
Pour the fruit juice over the currants and sugar. Leave it to soak, stirring occasionally.	Add the citrus peel and flaked almonds to the dry mixture. Stir well.
Warm the oven to 190°C/375°F (Gas Mark 5).	Lightly oil a 23cm×33cm (9 inch×13 inch) cake tin.
Add the soaked currants and juice to the dry mixture and stir slowly.	

Spread the batter into the tin and bake for 40 minutes at 190°C/375°F (Gas Mark 5). Allow the cake to cool before tipping it out of the tin. Serve as it is or with Meltability Sauce (page 99).

Answer: Because he lived on Baker Street.

SWEET BRIAR BREAD

The sweet briar rose has scented leaves which you can smell after a summer rain, flowers in June or July, and grows by itself on open ground, or tangled up in hedgerows. People have used the sweet briar for many centuries as medicinal food — both the petals and the 'hips' are edible. This sweet bread is made with a twist like its trailing stems, and a dollop of fruit preserves as its blossom. You might look for its 'hips' next time you walk out in the country: they are bright red and the birds love them. Allow 30 minutes for preparation, 30 minutes rising time, and 20 minutes cooking time. This recipe makes enough for 2 adults and 4 children.

285ml (½ pint) of tepid water 455g (1lb) of wholewheat flour 115g (4oz) of raw cane sugar	15ml (1 tablespoon) of dried yeast 5ml (1 teaspoon) of ground cinnamon 30ml (2 tablespoons) of soya oil 1 egg 225g (8oz) of fruit preserves

Measure 285ml (½ pint) of tepid water into a small jug.	Weigh out the flour into a large mixing bowl.
Add 15ml (1 tablespoon) of the sugar and yeast to the water. Stir well and leave to rise.	Add the cinnamon to the flour and stir.
Mix the soya oil, egg and the remaining sugar together in a small bowl.	Lightly oil a baking tray.
	When the yeast has risen, pour it over the flour mixture.
Add the oil, egg and sugar mix also. Stir well with a wooden spoon.	
Cover the dough and let it rise in a warm place for 10 minutes.	
	Lightly flour a board and turn out the dough.
Knead the dough and ...	break off small portions. Roll them into short, thick oblongs.

Fold each oblong in half and keep hold of the centre point. Now pull slightly as you twist the two ends around one another.

Warm the oven to 190°C/375°F (Gas Mark 5).	Place the twists onto the tray with some space between them. Arrange them into curved 'sweet briar' stems.
Cover the tray with a clean cloth and leave them to rise for 20 minutes.	
	Press your thumb into the centre end of each 'stem'.
Bake the 'stems' for 20 minutes at 190°C/375°F (Gas Mark 5).	
Remove the 'stems' from the oven and cool them on racks.	
	Drop some of the fruit preserve onto each of your thumbprints.
Serve these sweet briar breads immediately.	

BEAR-PAW CAKE

Not a *real* bear-paw! This is the name given to a kind of snowshoe: a round wooden or aluminium frame with nylon lacing criss-crossing it. 'Bear paws' are worn over shoes to prevent people from sinking into deep snow. This cake is very light and deep, like snow, with a 'bear-paw' pattern of carob on the top. Allow 20 minutes preparation and 1 hour cooking time. This recipe will make a cake big enough to fill 2 adults and 2 children *twice*.

115g (4oz) of raw cane sugar 2 eggs 115g (4oz) of margarine or butter 455g (1lb) of 81% flour	10ml (2 teaspoons) of baking powder 285ml (½ pint) of milk (soya or cow's) The juice of one orange 55g (2oz) of carob flake A deep, round cake tin

---

Weigh the sugar into a large mixing bowl.	Break one egg into a small bowl and pick out any bits of shell.
Add the margarine or butter to the sugar and use a fork to rub the two evenly together.	Pour that egg into a jug and break the second egg in the same way. Pour it into the jug.
Weigh out the flour and stir the baking powder in with it. Put aside.	Pour the milk into the jug with the eggs and whisk them together.
Slice an orange in half and squeeze the juice from it. Put it aside.	Keep whisking!
Warm the oven to 180°C/350°F (Gas Mark 4)	Pour the milk and egg in with the sugar and butter. Stir them together to a light, fluffy texture using a fork or whisk.
Add the flour mix to the egg and sugar mix a little bit at a time. Stir the mixture well between each addition to prevent lumps.	Lightly oil a deep, round cake tin and lightly flour the bottom.
	Pour the batter into the prepared cake tin and spread it to the edges.

Place the carob flakes in a criss-cross pattern on the top of the cake batter.

Pour the orange juice over the top of the cake.

Use a table knife to 'slice' the carob flakes and orange juice into the batter. This will create the lattice pattern deep into the cake.

Bake at 180°C/350°F (Gas Mark 4) for 55 minutes. Take it from the oven and allow it to cool on a rack for 10 minutes before removing it from the tin.

ALMOST PRETZELS

These bread sticks are twisted into the shape of crossed arms, a very old method of shaping bread which is meant to bring luck, or at least make a wish come true. Allow 1½ hours, including cooking and cooling. This serves 2 adults and 4 children. While they are baking, think of a wish. When they have cooked, take hold of one half of a pretzel and give the other half to someone else. Now pull. The person whose half includes the knot in the middle has their wish come true.

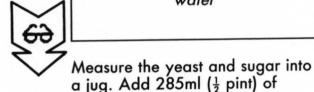

15ml (1 tablespoon) of dried yeast	455g (1lb) of wholewheat flour
15ml (1 tablespoon) of raw cane sugar	55g (2oz) of poppy, caraway or sesame seeds
570ml (1 pint) of tepid water	1 egg
	15ml (1 tablespoon) of milk (soya or cows)

Measure the yeast and sugar into a jug. Add 285ml (½ pint) of tepid water and stir.	Weigh the flour into a mixing bowl.
Measure the seeds into the flour.	Mix the egg and milk into a small bowl.
When the yeast has softened, pour it over the flour in the mixing bowl. Begin to stir it into the flour.	
	Gradually add the other 285ml (½ pint) of tepid water to the flour. Stir this well.
Begin to knead the dough, adding more water if necessary to make a firm dough.	
	Cover the dough with a clean cloth and leave it to rise for 20 minutes or until double in size.
Lightly flour a board and turn the dough out onto it. Knead well to reduce it in size again. Divide it into 5cm (2 inch) balls.	

Take each ball and roll it out into a thin 'string' about 30cm (12 inches) long. Now shape each 'string' into crossed arms and place on a baking tray.

Brush some of the egg and milk mix onto each 'almost pretzel'.

Warm the oven to 180°C/350°F (Gas Mark 4).

Cover them again and let them rise for another 20 minutes.

Bake the 'almost pretzels' for 30 minutes at 180°C/350°F (Gas Mark 4). Cool them on racks and serve the same day.

VAMPIRE BREAD

A few hundred years ago, in some parts of Europe, people were so frightened of vampires that they wore rings, necklaces and garlands of garlic to turn a vampire away. Some even slept with wreaths of garlic around their neck. This is a rich bread filled with an 'anti-vampire' mixture for all peace-loving people. Make it nearly a meal in itself by serving it with salad, soups or dips. This takes only 20 minutes to prepare and another 40 minutes to rise and cook. The amount here will help 2 adults and 2 children to ward off any other dubious characters as well.

15ml (1 tablespoon) of dried yeast	1 large egg
30ml (2 tablespoons) of raw cane sugar	30ml (2 tablespoons) of soya oil
140ml ($\frac{1}{4}$ pint) of tepid water	1 large onion
455g (1lb) of wholewheat flour	4 cloves of garlic
285ml ($\frac{1}{2}$ pint) of milk (soya or cow's)	A little soya oil
	115g (4oz) of stoned olives
	Rolling pin

Measure the yeast and sugar into a jug with $\frac{1}{4}$ pint of tepid water.	Weigh out the flour into a large mixing bowl.
Allow the yeast to soften and froth.	Mix the milk, egg and oil together in a jug. Stir well.
Pour the soft yeast into the bowl with the flour and begin to stir, using a large spoon.	
	Pour the milk, egg and oil mix over the flour also and stir well with the spoon.
Knead the dough very well to a firm ball. Cover it and put it aside to rise.	
Chop the onion and crush the garlic. Sauté them together in a small pan with a little soya oil until brown.	Drain the olives and slice each one into quarters.

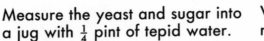

Lightly flour a board and find a rolling pin.

Roll the dough out on the board to 1cm ($\frac{3}{8}$ inch) thick. Cut it into 10cm (4 inch) circles.

Add the olives to the onions and stir well.

Warm the oven to 180°C/350°F (Gas Mark 4).

Spread the onion and olive mix over half of each cut-out and fold the dough over the filling.

Place the breads on a baking tray.

Allow the breads to rise for 20 minutes.

Bake them for 20 minutes at 180°C/350°F (Gas Mark 4). Serve warm.

WALNUT WINKS

The walnut is an 'eye' that winks out from this date and coconut 'face'.
These wholefood biscuits are chilled rather than baked and make excellent
freezer stuffers. You will need to make plenty — this makes 2 dozen — as
they disappear in just another wink. This recipe takes 45 minutes to
prepare. Then chill the winks for an hour, or deep-freeze them for lunch-
box treats.

225g (8oz) of dried dates	2.5ml (½ teaspoon) of
225g (8oz) of rolled oats	ground cinnamon
570ml (1 pint) of hot water	2.5ml (½ teaspoon) of
225g (8oz) of shredded coconut	ground cloves
	55g (2oz) of ground walnuts
	55g (2oz) of whole walnuts

Rinse the dates and pick out any stalks or pips.	Measure the oats into a large mixing bowl.
Chop the dates quite finely and place them in a bowl. Cover them with the hot water and put to one side.	Add half the shredded coconut to the oats in the bowl. Now add the ground cinnamon and ground cloves. Stir well.
Stir the dates to encourage them to soften.	Add the ground walnuts to the dry mix and stir.
Pour the dates and the water they soak in over the dry mix in the bowl. Stir this together very well.	Pick over the whole walnuts to remove any shell or debris.
Measure the remaining shredded coconut into a small bowl.	Spread greaseproof paper on a tray or worktop.
Take spoonsful of the mixture and mould them into balls with your hands.	Roll each 'wink' in the shredded coconut in the small bowl.

Place them on the greaseproof paper and press a walnut half into the
centre of each. Place the tray of 'winks' into the refrigerator and chill
for 1 hour. Eat these within two days or deep-freeze them
immediately.

SPICEY KISSES

Just what every cook needs after slaving away at the kitchen stove! These are crisp and rich for special occasions like Christmas or Easter, or just for doing a good job. This recipe will make 2 dozen. They take only 20 minutes to prepare and 12 minutes to cook. Idea: see what objects there are around your house for use as cutters to give interesting shapes to these kisses.

55g (2oz) of margarine or *butter*	2.5ml (½ teaspoon) of caraway seed
115g (4oz) of honey (or *icing sugar*)	2.5ml (½ teaspoon) of ground cumin
15ml (1 tablespoon) of milk (*soya or cow's*)	2.5ml (½ teaspoon) of ground cloves
225g (8oz) of wholewheat flour	Rolling pin and cutters

Weigh the margarine or butter into a mixing bowl.	Weigh the honey (or icing sugar) into the mixing bowl with the margarine.
Use a fork and blend the honey and butter together. Add the milk as you continue blending.	Weigh the flour into a bowl.
Warm the oven to 190°C/375°F (Gas Mark 5).	Add the caraway, cumin and cloves to the flour. Stir well.
Gradually add the flour mixture to the butter and sugar mix, stirring with the fork all the while.	
	Roll the dough out onto a board with the rolling pin.

Using any sort of cutter, cut shapes from the dough and place them on baking trays. Bake each trayful for 12 minutes at 190°C/375°F (Gas Mark 5). Re-roll the dough that remains and continue cutting and baking until all is used. Cool the 'kisses' on racks.

6. COOKER-TOP SPECIALS

FLAPPERS!

This name was given to some young women who, in the 1920s, were able to cause a commotion or a 'flap' by the way they dressed and behaved. These flapjacks will do the same if you top them to suit any meal of the day. This recipe makes 2 dozen 10cm (4 inch) flappers. You will need only 15 minutes to mix the batter and 10 minutes to cook each batch. The toppings need only 10 minutes preparation time.

425ml ($\frac{3}{4}$ pint) of milk
(soya or cow's)
1 egg
455g (1lb) of wholewheat
flour
7.5ml (1$\frac{1}{2}$ teaspoons) of
baking powder
30ml (2 tablespoons) of soya oil

*

BREAKFAST TOPPING
115g (4oz) of 'runny' honey
55g (2oz) of margarine
or butter
5ml (1 teaspoon) of
ground cinnamon

MIDDAY TOPPING
30ml (2 tablespoons) of finely
chopped chives
30ml (2 tablespoons) of finely
chopped parsley
225g (8oz) of natural yogurt

*

DINNER TOPPING
1 medium onion
2 cloves of garlic
A little soya oil
225g (8oz) of cheese
115g (4oz) of olives

Measure the milk into a jug with the egg. Whisk them together with a fork.

Weigh the flour into a bowl. Add the baking powder and stir well.

Pour the liquid over the flour and stir with a fork, then a large spoon. The mixture should be quite moist and slightly bubbly. Set aside.

Decide which topping to make. (You may prepare it while the batter sets.)

For Breakfast: Measure the honey and margarine or butter into a bowl. Stir together.

Add the ground cinnamon to the mix. Stir well and spoon over the hot flappers.

For Midday: Wash and finely chop the chives and parsley.

Mix the herbs into the yogurt and spoon over the hot flappers. Garnish with parsley.

For Dinner: Peel and grate one onion and two cloves of garlic. Sauté them together in a little oil.

Grate the cheese.

Slice the olives.

Mix the onion, garlic, cheese and olives together and spread between the hot flappers.

Rub a little of the oil onto a griddle or frying pan. Heat the pan until very hot and then drop large spoonsful of the batter onto it.

Warm the plates in the oven.

Watch the batter cook until you notice the upper side bubbling.

Use a spatula to lift and flip the flappers onto their other side.

Lift one edge of the flapper to see if the under side is brown. Then lift it and serve.

It is best to serve two or three flappers to each person at once. With topping in between each flapper, you get *layers* of flavour. If you wish, you may keep the flappers warm in the oven until you want to serve them.

SEEDS FOR THE SOWERS

Seeds aren't just for the birds. People have been eating them too, for as long as there have been people. Seeds are little storehouses of nutrients. They are harvested just before, or as, they are ready to ripen and fall. Some are even able to lie dormant for many years until conditions are right for them to grow into plants. That is why land that has been newly turned, such as building sites, produces a crop of plants which may not have been seen for years. The seeds in this dish give all of their goodness to you. This recipe is for 2 adults and 2 children. You will need 40 minutes to complete the dish.

1 litre (approx. 2 pints) of water	10ml (2 teaspoons) of mustard seeds
455g (1lb) of millet or rice	10ml (2 teaspoons) of sesame seeds
15ml (1 tablespoon) of olive oil	2 onions
55g (2oz) of pumpkin seeds	$\frac{1}{4}$ of a white cabbage
170g (6oz) of sunflower seeds	2 oranges
55g (2oz) of cashew nuts	5ml (1 teaspoon) of thyme or marjoram
10ml (2 teaspoons) of poppy seeds	5ml (1 teaspoon) of paprika
10ml (2 teaspoons) of celery seeds	

Bring the water to the boil in a saucepan.	Measure the millet or rice into a sieve and rinse well.
Add the millet or rice to the water and simmer over a low heat for 25 minutes stirring occasionally.	Pour the olive oil into a large frying pan.
Place the pan over a low heat and add the pumpkin and sunflower seeds. Now add the cashew nuts.	Measure the poppy, celery, mustard and sesame seeds into the frying pan.
Peel and thinly slice the onions and add them to the frying pan.	Use a wooden spoon to stir the mixture in the frying pan.
Begin to shred the cabbage. Place it to one side.	Keep stirring!

Carefully peel the oranges and save the peels. Pick off any pith and then divide the oranges into their segments.

Measure out the thyme (or marjoram) and paprika into the mixture in the frying pan.

Cut some decorative shapes from the orange peel. Put to one side.

When the onions are browned, add the orange segments and the shredded cabbage.

Drain any remaining liquid from the rice or millet and fluff it up with a fork.

Change hands but keep stirring!

Spoon some rice or millet onto each of four plates, pushing it out towards the edges of the plate.

Spoon some of the seed mixture over the rice or millet.

Garnish the serving with the orange peel shapes.

Serve immediately with some tamari or shoyu near at hand if a salty flavour is preferred.

FLIES IN THE BUTTERMILK

Buttermilk is the milk that is drained away from freshly made butter. It is rich and cream-coloured, with tiny lumps of butter floating in it and flies aren't the only creatures who love it. Real buttermilk is good for making cakes and breads as well as just drinking. In this dish the milk is the thin milk, the rice is the rich milk, the cheese chunks are the lumps of butter, and the currants are the flies. There is enough here for 2 adults and 2 children. Allow 40 minutes total. Note: it is not a good idea to eat *real* flies, or to let them get into your food.

1 litre (approx 2 pints) of water 455g (1lb) of brown or Basmati rice 115g (4oz) of currants	225g (8oz) of Cheddar cheese 570ml (1 pint) of milk (soya or cow's) Sea salt and freshly ground black pepper to taste

Bring the water to the boil in a saucepan.	Wash the Basmati or brown rice in a sieve.
Add the rice to the water and allow it to simmer for 25–30 minutes.	Rinse and pick over the currants.
Weigh out the cheese and cut it into small cubes.	Pour the milk into a serving jug.
Drain any liquid from the rice.	
	Stir the currants into the cooked rice.
Stir the cubes of cheese into the rice and cover the pan while you prepare brightly coloured bowls.	
Serve immediately, pouring a little milk over each serving. Add salt and pepper to taste.	

PIPESTONE PORRIDGE

Pipestone is a place as well as a stone. The stone, which is reddish brown, was used by the North American Indians to make 'peace-pipes'. The place was possibly the site of peace councils held between many different Indian tribes. The fiery chilli and the subtle orange flavours in this dish blend with the peaceful flavour and colour of red lentils — the easiest lentil to cook, and I think the prettiest. This will make enough for 2 adults and 2 children. Allow 45 minutes for preparation and cooking.

1.5 litres (approx. 3 pints) of water	15ml (1 tablespoon) of soya oil
455g (1lb) of red lentils	2.5ml ($\frac{1}{2}$ teaspoon) of chilli powder
2 oranges	140g (5oz) of tomato paste
1 large onion	

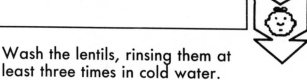

Pour the water into a large saucepan. Place over high heat.	Wash the lentils, rinsing them at least three times in cold water.
Add the lentils to the water, boil and then allow them to simmer for 25 minutes, stirring often.	Wash the oranges and slice them into halves.
Peel and slice the onions and gently sauté in the oil.	Measure out the chilli powder.
Add the tomato paste to the sautéed onions. Now add the chilli. Stir well and bring to a gentle simmer.	Squeeze three of the orange halves and add the juice to the tomato and onion sauce. Stir.
When the lentils are soft to the bite, remove them from the heat and add the tomato sauce. Stir well.	Slice the remaining orange half into thin rounds.

Ladle the lentil porridge into bowls. Place one of the orange slices onto each portion and serve immediately.

EGGS IS EGGS

There is a saying, 'sure as eggs is eggs', to describe something that is a certainty or about which one has no doubts. This eggcellent dish works every time — just keep your plates hot and serve it up immediately it has finished cooking. This will make enough for 2 adults *or* 4 children. It takes 15 minutes to prepare and 10 minutes to cook.

1 small onion 1 medium carrot 2 large lettuce leaves 115g (4oz) of Cheddar cheese 15ml (1 tablespoon) of fresh tarragon	5ml (1 teaspoon) of freshly ground black pepper 2 large eggs 45ml (3 tablespoons) of milk (soya or cow's) A little soya oil

Peel and shred the onion.	Scrub the carrot.
Grate the carrot quite finely and put it in a bowl together with the shredded onion.	Wash the lettuce leaves. Shake the water from them.
Slice the lettuce leaves very thinly, about 1cm ($\frac{3}{8}$ inch) wide.	Grate the cheese and put to one side.
Measure out the tarragon and pepper and add to the onion and carrot.	Break one egg into a small bowl and pick out any pieces of shell.
Stir those together, but keep the cheese and lettuce separate.	Pour that egg into a jug with the milk. Add the second egg in the same way.
Spread the oil in a large frying pan and place it over a medium heat.	Whisk the egg and milk to a froth with a fork.
Pour the egg and milk mixture into the pan.	Find the lid to the frying pan.
Sprinkle the carrot and onion mix over the egg, pushing it to the edges.	
	Spread the sliced lettuce leaves over the carrot and onion mixture.

Sprinkle the grated cheese over the lettuce and place the cover on the pan.

 Allow the eggs to cook for 7–10 minutes. Remove the lid and slice the 'eggs-is-eggs' into halves or quarters. Lift out the portions with a spatula. Serve immediately with salad or cooked vegetables.

RED AND GINGER DUET

There are a lot of strong personalities in this casserole but they perform really well together. The overall colour is red, the flavour is earthy with a ginger bite, and the texture is enough to make anyone start tapping. You will have to think ahead to make this dish but then it will only take one hour for preparation and cooking. There is enough here for 2 adults and 2 children.

225g (8oz) of dried chick peas 455g (1lb) of green grapes 2 medium onions 2 medium beetroot	15ml (1 tablespoon) of soya oil 5ml (1 teaspoon) of ground ginger A pressure cooker

Wash and then soak the chick peas in cold water overnight or all day.

Drain the water from the chick peas and place them in the pressure cooker with a little water. Cook for about 20 minutes at pressure.	Wash the grapes and pull them from the stalks. Cut each one in half along its length and scrape away the seeds.
Peel and chop the onions.	Scrub the beetroot.
Grate the beetroot. Your hands will get stained a bright red!	Pour the soya oil into a large saucepan.
Heat the oil over a medium heat and sauté the onions in it. Stir often.	Add the ginger to the onions. Stir well.
Add the cooked chick peas to the onion and stir often to brown them slightly.	
	Add the grated beetroot to the saucepan and stir well.
Now add the grape halves. Stir well, cover and leave to cook for 10 minutes.	

Serve this immediately — on its own or over rice.

PULLET SURPRISE

A Pullet is a young hen. Her eggs are usually a little smaller than those of older hens and they also have a slightly stronger taste.

Prepare your side dishes beforehand as this takes only 10 minutes to prepare and 5 minutes to cook. This is enough for 2 adults *or* 4 children .

> 1 small onion
> 3 small eggs
> 140ml ($\frac{1}{4}$ pint) of milk
> (soya or cow's)
> A little soya oil
> 7g ($\frac{1}{4}$oz) of mixed, fresh herbs
>
> (parsley, basil, thyme)
> 115g (4oz) of Cheddar cheese
> 1 small green pepper
> 55g (2oz) of broken
> cashew nuts

Peel and finely chop one onion.	Whisk the eggs and milk in a jug.
Sauté the onion in a little soya oil over a low heat.	Wash the fresh herbs you have selected for use. Chop finely.
Wash and dice one small pepper.	Grate the cheese.
Weigh out the cashew nuts.	Pour the egg and milk mixture into the pan with the onions and spread it to the edges.
Spread the diced pepper and herbs over the eggs.	Add the cashew pieces.
Use a spatula to lift the edges of the cooking egg after 2 minutes.	
	Sprinkle the grated cheese over the egg mixture.
Fold the egg in on itself: one edge towards the centre, the other folded to meet the first.	
Leave it to cook for another 2 minutes then lift it from the pan onto a hot platter and cut into two or four pieces.	
	Garnish with more fresh herbs or fresh tomato slices.
Serve immediately with salad or hot vegetables.	

7. SPREADS AND SAUCES

THE BED SPREAD

OK — I know that eating in bed is against all the rules, especially after you've brushed your teeth. This thick spread is specially engineered to make sure that drips and spills don't give you away. Use it in sandwiches, on cake, toast or carrot. Takes only 10 minutes to prepare and makes enough for two healthy servings, whenever you decide to use it.

15ml (1 tablespoon) fresh mint *One very ripe banana* *15ml (1 tablespoon) of tahini*	*30ml (2 tablespoons) natural* *yogurt* *(or sour cream or tofu)*

Chop the mint very finely.	Peel the banana and use a fork to mash it in a bowl.
Prepare whatever you are going to spread this on.	Add the tahini, mint and yogurt to the mashed banana and stir well so the mixture is smooth and light.

Serve ready-spread or in a separate dish with a sprig of mint as garnish.

MIGHTY MOUTH DRESSING

If the mustard doesn't get you the garlic will. But, just in time, the honey smothers the flames and smoothes this dressing into an all-time great. I use it with many different dishes: salads, baked potatoes, mushrooms on toast and so on. This makes 285ml ($\frac{1}{2}$ pint) and takes only 10 minutes to prepare.

2 cloves of garlic	5ml (1 teaspoon) of dried thyme
15ml (1 tablespoon) of honey	45ml (3 tablespoons) of soya oil
10ml (2 teaspoons) of dry mustard	200ml ($\frac{1}{3}$ pint) of cider or wine vinegar

Peel the garlic cloves and crush them into a jug or large jar.	Measure the honey into the jug or jar.
Add the mustard and thyme to the mixture.	Pour the soya oil into the jug or jar.
Pour the vinegar into the jug or jar.	

Stir or shake the mixture for 2 or 3 minutes to create an emulsion. Use immediately or store in the refrigerator for up to two days.

BETTER-THAN GRAVY

This really is better than any other sort of gravy. It is rich and dark and will stand up to the most critical taste-buds at any Sunday lunch, Christmas dinner or Thanksgiving Day Feast. This makes approximately 570ml (1 pint) and takes only 20 minutes to prepare.

1 large onion	*1 slice of wholewheat bread*
2 cloves of garlic	*1 bay-leaf*
A little soya oil	*140ml (5 fl oz) of apple juice*
425ml ($\frac{3}{4}$ pint) of vegetable stock	
(see page 17)	

Peel and finely chop one large onion and two cloves of garlic. Sauté them in the soya oil over a medium heat.

Pour 425ml ($\frac{3}{4}$ pint) of vegetable stock into a jug.

Pour 30ml (2 tablespoons) of vegetable stock over the onion and garlic. Stir well.

Crumble the bread slice over the onions. Add the bay-leaf.

Allow the onion, garlic and bread crumbs to brown and thicken as you stir. Add more of the stock gradually.

Measure the apple juice into a jug and place to one side.

When all of the stock has been added, pour in the apple juice and let the gravy simmer for another 5 minutes.

Serve the gravy immediately in a china gravy-boat or jug.

TURTLE RIVER SPREAD

The Turtle River is in northern Minnesota — a few miles from Bemidji, home of the giant Paul Bunyan. That whole area is a network of lakes and rivers where there really *are* turtles in abundance. Keeping very still, one can watch them basking in the sun with their necks stretched as far out of their shells as possible. A sudden movement will send them diving — plop — into the water for safety. I first made this spread while on a canoe trip on the Turtle River, so I used tinned peas and tofu. But you could as easily use fresh peas and yogurt. This recipe makes enough for 2 adults and 2 children. It takes only 15 minutes to prepare. Note: although the colour of this spread may resemble turtles, *no* turtles are included in it.

455g (1lb) of cooked peas	15ml (1 tablespoon) of fresh mint
285g (10oz) of tofu or yogurt	(or 5ml (1 teaspoon) of dried)
1 small shredded onion	5ml (1 teaspoon) of paprika

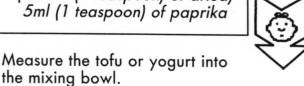

Drain the liquid from the peas and place them in a mixing bowl.	Measure the tofu or yogurt into the mixing bowl.
Peel and shred a small onion quite finely. Add it to the mixing bowl.	Mix the peas, tofu and onion together using a fork.
Wash the mint and chop it finely. Add it to the pea mixture.	Continue to mash and stir the pea mixture.
Measure out the paprika and add it to the mixing bowl.	
	Complete the mixing after all the ingredients have been added and the spread is an even consistency.

Serve immediately in sandwiches, on crackers or with raw vegetables.

SMOKEY BEAR DRESSING

'Smokey' is a cartoon bear used by the US Forest Rangers to advertise safe use of fire while camping or travelling through wooded areas. He wears a broad-rimmed hat and says 'Only YOU can prevent forest fires'. You will need him after you've tried this fiery sauce! This makes 285ml (½ pint) of dressing and takes only 10 minutes to prepare. Serve it with salads, baked potatoes, rice dishes or barbecues.

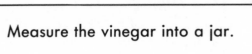

1 small fresh chilli 140ml (5fl oz) of wine or cider vinegar 1 lemon	90ml (3fl oz) of olive oil 5ml (1 teaspoon) of mustard seeds

Wash and finely chop one small fresh chilli.	Measure the vinegar into a jar.
Slice the lemon in half and squeeze the juice from it. Add the juice to the vinegar in the jar.	Add the olive oil to the vinegar.
Add the chopped chilli to the vinegar and oil.	Measure the mustard seeds and add to the vinegar and oil mix.
Place the lid on the jar and shake the mixture very well.	
Serve immediately or chill for 30 minutes.	

MELTABILITY SAUCE

This sauce is sweet, a little bit tangy, and doesn't hang around for very long. It sets firm if refrigerated, spreads easily on bread or crackers, warms into a liquid sauce for cakes and waffles, and generally has that melt-in-your-mouth quality that ensures its place on your list of 'greats'. It makes about 570ml (1 pint) of sauce and will keep, *hidden* in the refrigerator, for 3–4 days. Allow 15 minutes preparation time.

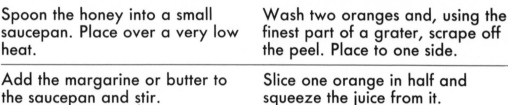

225g (8oz) of honey	5ml (1 teaspoon) of ground cinnamon
Peel from 2 oranges	
115g (4oz) of margarine or butter	2.5ml ($\frac{1}{2}$ teaspoon) of ground nutmeg
Juice from 1 orange	115g (4oz) of ground nuts

Spoon the honey into a small saucepan. Place over a very low heat.	Wash two oranges and, using the finest part of a grater, scrape off the peel. Place to one side.
Add the margarine or butter to the saucepan and stir.	Slice one orange in half and squeeze the juice from it.
When the honey and butter have melted, add the orange juice to the saucepan and stir well.	Add the cinnamon and nutmeg to the sauce.
Add the ground nuts to the saucepan.	Add the grated orange peel to the saucepan.

Stir very well and leave warming while you prepare the servings. Serve immediately over cake, waffles, etc., or pour into a heatproof jug, cover and chill for use later.

WHITE-WATEΓ DIP

White-water is the frothy, rough water that passes rapidly over a shallow piece of riverbed. It is very pretty to look at and pretty exciting to float through. This dip has the same colour and speckled texture as a white-water. Eat it with raw vegetables, pieces of toast or just your finger. This will be enough for 2 adults and 2 children and takes only 10 minutes to prepare.

285g (10oz) of soft tofu *10ml (2 teaspoons) of* *dill seeds*	*30ml (2 tablespoons) of tahini* *10ml (2 teaspoons) of tamari* *or shoyu*

Drain the tofu and mash it with a fork into a small mixing bowl.	Measure out the dill seeds and pick out any stalks. Add the dill to the tofu.
Pour the tahini into the bowl with the tofu.	
	Add the tamari to the mixture and stir very well using a fork.
Add more tahini or tamari to taste if necessary.	
Stir very well and serve immediately or chill it for 30 minutes.	

LOON BUTTER

A loon is a really weird bird. It has a goofy song and even goofier habits. It gets up at four o'clock every morning, brushes its beak, then sings an eerie song, then does a quick circle-dance, and finally dives into icy cold water. This spread is called after the loon because, just like the bird's lifestyle, it is an unusual mixture of ingredients. Allow 15 minutes to prepare enough for 4 children.

115g (4oz) of margarine or butter	*15ml (1 tablespoon) of lemon juice*
10ml (2 teaspoons) of dried mustard	*10ml (2 teaspoons) of poppy seed*

Measure the butter or margarine into a small mixing bowl.	Measure the mustard and add to the butter or margarine.
Squeeze the juice from a lemon and pour 15ml (1 tablespoon) in with the butter/margarine and mustard.	Add the poppy seed to the mixing bowl.

Use a fork to stir the contents of the bowl together to a light consistency. Taste it and adjust the ingredients to suit your taste.

Serve immediately on bread or crackers. In sandwiches, add layers of cress or tomato. This butter will keep for one week in the fridge.

BARBARA CUTE SAUCE

A very young friend misunderstood me to say this when talking to her mother. It is a pleasing alternative to the original title, I think. The sauce is good with many foods, not just those which have been barbecued. This makes 1 litre (approx. 2 pints) — that's usually enough for 4 adults and 4 children. It will take 30 minutes to prepare.

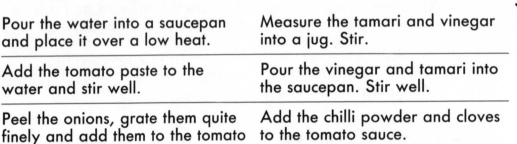

570ml (1 pint) of water
140ml (¼ pint) of tamari or shoyu
285ml (½ pint) of cider vinegar
285g (10oz) of tomato paste
2 small onions

2.5ml (½ teaspoon) of chilli powder
5ml (1 teaspoon) of ground cloves
3 cloves of garlic

Pour the water into a saucepan and place it over a low heat.	Measure the tamari and vinegar into a jug. Stir.
Add the tomato paste to the water and stir well.	Pour the vinegar and tamari into the saucepan. Stir well.
Peel the onions, grate them quite finely and add them to the tomato sauce. Stir well.	Add the chilli powder and cloves to the tomato sauce.
	Peel the garlic cloves and crush them into the sauce.

Allow the sauce to simmer gently for 20 minutes stirring occasionally.

Use this sauce immediately with beans, root vegetables, 'Bundles of Sticks', etc. Or chill it and store it in the refrigerator for up to two days.

MAKE IN HASTE PASTE

This spread is a quick *pâté par excellence* for your weekend picnic or 'forgot-they-were-coming' visitors. It is said that the sign of a good cook is one who can produce an impromptu something special. Here's your chance to prove it. The recipe makes enough for 2 adults and 2 children, and takes 20 minutes to prepare.

285g (10oz) of cooked beans (any sort) 1 ripe banana 30ml (2 tablespoons) of tahini 1 large carrot 1 small onion	Freshly ground black pepper to taste 90ml (3fl oz) of any fruit juice A food processor

Measure the beans into a food processor.	Peel the banana and place it in the food processor with the beans.
Add the tahini to the beans and banana.	Scrub the carrot and chop it into large chunks.
Peel and quarter the onion.	
	Add the carrot, onion and ground pepper to the bean and banana mix.
Pour the fruit juice into the processor with the beans, banana, carrot and onion.	
Draw a straw to see who gets to:	press the button to pureé the mixture to an even consistency.

Serve immediately on bread, crackers or raw vegetables, or press into a dish, garnish and chill for 30 minutes before serving.

BELLS OF WHITECHAPEL SAUCE

Two sticks and an apple
Say the Bells of Whitechapel.

This is the seventh stanza in the song 'The Bells of London'. It is a very old and very well-known song about fourteen bells in Old London Town. The sticks in this recipe are large spring onions but there is a real apple. Use as an excellent dressing for garden fresh salads, or try floating some into your favourite soup. Who knows the rest of the song?

340g (12oz) of natural yogurt	1 eating apple
2 very large spring onions	A food processor

Pour the yogurt into the food processor.

'Top and tail' two very large spring onions and add them to the food processor.

Wash and quarter one eating apple. Carefully remove the core from each piece.

Now peel the apple quarters and add them to the food processor.

(Make sure the lid is on.)

Press the button. Purée until the mixture is very smooth.

Serve immediately on salads, soups or baked potatoes. You may chill it for use later the same day.

8. SNACKS & TREATS

HEDGEHOG ON A LOG

Every day after school was out, I and my eight brothers and sisters would invade our kitchen and ransack the cupboards for the weirdest snack we could devise. This was one of the most sensible concoctions! The celery is the log, the peanut butter and yeast stuffing is the hedgehog, and the sunflower seeds are his prickles. Two kids can finish off this amount in less time than it takes to make — and that's only 5 minutes.

4 stalks of celery 30ml (2 tablespoons) of peanut butter	15ml (1 tablespoon) of yeast extract 115g (4oz) of sunflower seeds

Read the newspaper.

Wash the celery really well. Use a vegetable brush to get the stubborn dirt off.

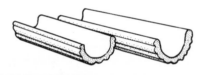

Slice the stalks of celery into 7–10cm (3–4 inch) pieces. Let the stalks dry while you mix the 'hedgehog'.

Pour a cup of tea.

Measure the peanut butter and yeast extract into a small bowl. Use a fork to beat them to a smooth, fluffy texture.

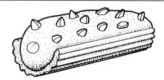

Now press some 'hedgehog' mixture into the hollow of each slice of celery. Really fill up the hollow — or even *over* fill it.

Ask for a sample.

Next, spread the sunflower seeds onto a plate. Roll the 'log' so that the seeds stick to the 'hedgehog'. Serve.

FRUITY GOOP

The Goops they lick their fingers,
the Goops they lick their knives.
They spill their broth on the tablecloth
and lead disgusting lives!*

Are you a Goop yet? If you're not, this fruity treat is sure to turn you into one. In 15 minutes you can prepare enough for 2 adults and 2 children to become entirely goopy. Idea — try drawing some Goops, before and after they become Goopified.

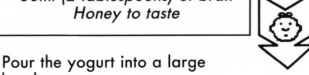

340g (12oz) of natural yogurt	115g (4oz) of raisins
2 apples or pears	15g ($\frac{1}{2}$oz) of fresh, chopped mint
2 oranges	55g (2oz) of dates
1 grapefruit	30ml (2 tablespoons) of bran
1 banana	Honey to taste

Wash the apples/pears.	Pour the yogurt into a large bowl.
Chop the apples/pears; peel and chop the oranges and grapefruit. Add them all to the yogurt.	Peel the banana and slice it into circles. Add the banana to the yogurt.
	Weigh out the raisins. Wash them and then add them to the yogurt mixture.
Wash and chop the mint. Stir it in with the fruit and yogurt.	Chop the dates and add to the yogurt. Stir very well with a large spoon.

Now scoop some Fruity Goop into 4 small bowls. Sprinkle one dessert spoon of bran over each serving. Pour a bit of honey over the bran if you would like a bit more sweetness and serve.

* *Goops and How to Be Them*
A manual of manners for polite infants inculcating many juvenile virtues both by precept and example.
With 90 drawings, by Gelett Burgess.
(Dover Publications, New York. Distributed by Constable and Co, London.)

JUNE BUGS

In many parts of the world, giant beetles appear in May and June of each year. They are noisy and shiny and horrific looking but, so far as I know, entirely harmless. However, they *do* like to land on people's noses! Onlookers laugh hysterically while the 'victim' *screams* hysterically. These stuffed fresh dates resemble the beetles (only slightly) and get a good response - though not a hysterical one. This amount is usually enough for 2 adults and 2 children. It will take you 30 minutes to prepare.

455g (1lb) of fresh dates 170g (6oz) of cream cheese 5ml (1 teaspoon) of freshly ground coriander	115g (4oz) of natural yogurt 115g (4oz) of walnut halves

Wash the dates.	Weigh the cream cheese into a mixing bowl.
Slice each date in half. Remove the pip and any very dry pulp.	Add the coriander and yogurt to the cheese. Stir well using a fork or knife.
Overfill each date half with the cheese mixture.	
	Top each stuffed date with a walnut half. Pick only the most attractive walnuts and brush any husk from them.
Chill the June Bugs before serving on a brightly coloured plate.	

GOOBER BERRY BOWL

You know what a berry is, but can you think what a goober might be? It is thought to come from 'nguba', a word brought to the US by slaves from the Congo. Those slaves were settled in the southern states and worked on farms that grew … peanuts! And peanuts were called goobers or sometimes goober peas. This treat uses goober-butter and berries and makes enough for 2 adults and 2 children. You should allow 30 minutes preparation time and another 30 minutes for it to chill.

900g (2lb) of raspberries or blackberries	340g (12oz) of natural yogurt
8–12 slices of wholewheat bread	200ml (6fl oz) of any fruit juice
225g (8oz) of goober-butter (peanut butter)	55g (2oz) of ground goobers (peanuts)

Wash the berries. Place them in a colander to drain.

Spread each slice of bread with some goober butter and place to one side.

Put a handful of berries in the bottom of a deep casserole dish or bowl.

Mix the yogurt with the fruit juice. Stir well.

Place some of the bread slices over the berries, butter side up. Add another handful of berries and spread them evenly over the bread layer.

Now pour a bit of the yogurt and fruit juice mixture over the berries and spread it around.

Place another layer of sliced bread over the yogurt, butter side up.

Add another layer of berries, then another layer of yogurt.

Repeat these layers, finishing with a topping of yogurt. Sprinkle the ground goobers over the yogurt and chill for 30 minutes before serving.

TWIDDLES

Can you twiddle your thumbs? In different directions at the same time? These bread twists have twiddles in their middles — made of herbs and yeast extract. They are excellent after-school snacks for 4 children. Allow 30 minutes to prepare them, including cooking. If twiddling is too easy for you, try rubbing your stomach and patting your head at the same time — now change hands.

8 slices of wholewheat bread 115g (4oz) of margarine or butter 5ml (1 teaspoon) of dried sage	5ml (1 teaspoon) of dried thyme 2 cloves of garlic 30ml (2 tablespoons) of yeast extract

If you are using thick slices of bread, cut off their crusts and put them to one side (for use in Re-Baked Bread, page 72).

Measure the butter or margarine into a small bowl. Add the sage and thyme. Stir very well using a fork.

Peel and crush the garlic cloves. Add the garlic to the herb butter and stir well.

Warm the oven to 170°C/325°F (Gas Mark 3).

Spread some herb and garlic butter on one side of each bread slice.

Spread a thin layer of yeast extract on the other side of the bread slices.

Roll the bread slices tightly in on themselves, butter side out.

Press them onto a baking sheet, close together, with the rolled edge of the bread facing down.

Bake for 10 minutes at 170°C/325°F (Gas Mark 3). Serve immediately.

TORNADO CHILL

Tornados are funnel-shaped whirlwinds that come out of the clouds and flick their narrow 'tails' as they move rapidly along. Where I grew up, there were tornado warnings announced over radio and television. When the warning included our neighbourhood, we had to go into the basement (with lots of snacks!) and wait for the tornados to pass. Sometimes we even spent a night camping in the cellar. This treat has a 'tornado' of good things in its centre. It makes enough for 2 adults and 2 children. Allow 10 minutes to prepare, but you'll have to think about making this an hour before you want to serve it.

455g (16oz) of natural yogurt
115g (4oz) of ground nuts
115g (4oz) of shredded, unsweetened coconut

5ml (1 teaspoon) of ground nutmeg
60ml (4 tablespoons) of honey

Measure the yogurt evenly between four dessert bowls and place them in the freezer compartment of your fridge. Do this about 1 hour before you want to serve this snack.

Measure the ground nuts and coconut into a small bowl.

Add the nutmeg to the nut mixture and stir well.

Remove the nearly-frozen portions of yogurt from the freezer.

Pour 15ml (1 tablespoon) of honey over each portion.

Sprinkle a quarter of the nut mixture over the honey.

Using a table knife, stir the honey and nut topping swiftly into the icy yogurt so that you make a whirlwind right into the centre of the portion. Serve this immediately or re-chill for use a little later the same day.

WADING BIRDS SNACK

Have you ever wondered how those tall, skinny-legged, wading birds can stand up in water? In this snack, the water is the sauce, the birds are the vegetables, their skinny legs are the cocktail sticks and the underwater carrots are there to keep the birds balanced while they look at their elegant reflections. Allow 20 minutes to prepare enough for 2 adults *or* 4 children. Idea: complete the landscape by arranging a shrubbery of salad around the lake.

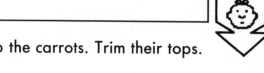

140ml (5fl oz) of cider vinegar 4 large carrots 60ml (2fl oz) of olive oil 455g (1lb) of button mushrooms 10ml (2 teaspoons) of tamari or shoyu	1 cucumber 5ml (1 teaspoon) of dried parsley 115g (4oz) of radishes Cocktail sticks

Measure the cider vinegar into a jug.	Scrub the carrots. Trim their tops.
Add the olive oil to the vinegar in the jug.	Wash the mushrooms and leave to drain.
Pour the tamari or shoyu into the oil and vinegar.	Wash the cucumber.
Sprinkle the parsley into the jug and stir the mixture well.	Wash the radishes and trim their tops and tails.
Select a broad, shallow dish and pour the vinegar sauce into it (the lake).	Slice the cucumber into thin circles and put to one side.
Cut the carrots into circles as thick as the 'lake' is deep.	Slice the radish into circles.

Make the 'birds' by piercing one cucumber slice, one radish slice and one whole mushroom and pushing these together near the top of the stick. Now push the other end of each stick into a carrot chunk. Immerse the carrot in the 'lake' of sauce, leaving just the 'wading bird' standing. Repeat until all of the vegetables, or the space in the 'lake', is used up.

VOYAGEURS' MUNCH

When the Europeans were exploring North America many years ago, there were men called *voyageurs* who transported food, clothing and other goods to small trading-posts. These men travelled by rivers and lakes in huge canoes which required great strength to paddle. They needed foods, such as this one, which were easy to eat while they were working. This mixture will keep your energy up while you imagine having to paddle miles each day. It will make enough for four and takes 10 minutes to prepare, 30 minutes to cook. Idea: find a map and see if you can get from one town to another by 'travelling' on water alone.

115g (4oz) of cashew nut pieces 170g (6oz) of rolled oats 55g (2oz) of wheat bran 55g (2oz) of caraway seed 60ml (4 tablespoons) of boiling water	170g (6oz) of sunflower seed 60 ml (4 tablespoons) of molasses A little soya oil

Measure out the cashew nut pieces and put them into a large bowl.	Weigh the rolled oats and pour them into the bowl.
Warm the oven to 170°C/325°F (Gas Mark 3).	Measure 55g (2oz) each of wheat bran and caraway seed and add them to the bowl.
Measure out the boiling water.	Weigh out the sunflower seeds and pour them into the bowl.
Add the boiled water to the molasses and stir well.	Stir the dry mixture very well. Lightly oil a baking tray.
Pour the molasses over the dry mix and stir very well with a large spoon.	
	Spread the mixture out onto the oiled baking tray.

Bake for 30 minutes at 170°C/325°F (Gas Mark 3). Stir the mixture once or twice so that it roasts evenly. Serve immediately in small bowls, or allow to cool and store in an airtight container.

FIREFLIES AND GLOW-WORMS

Both these amazing insects have a substance in their abdomen that causes them to be luminous at night. In fact, they are from the same family: the glow-worms are the wingless women and children, the fireflies have wings and are male. In this snack the popcorn kernels are the fireflies and the cheeses are the glow-worms. This recipe will light up 4 children and takes only 20 minutes to make.

15ml (1 tablespoon) of soya oil 115g (4oz) of Leicester cheese 85g (3oz) of popcorn kernels	5ml (1 teaspoon) of freshly ground black pepper (or paprika) 30g (1oz) of Parmesan cheese

Pour the soya oil into a large flat-bottomed saucepan and place it over a high heat.	Grate the Leicester cheese and place to one side.
When the oil is hot, add the popcorn kernels. Shake the pan from side to side and cover it. Now wait for the popping to begin.	Mix the pepper or paprika with the Parmesan cheese and put aside.
Continue to shake the pan when the popping starts, always holding it close to the heat.	Prepare a large bowl for the popped corn and a small bowl for each person.
Pour the popped corn into the large bowl as it rises to the top of the pan.	Add the grated cheese and the Parmesan mix to the popped corn a little at a time. Stir well after each addition.

Serve this immediately. The heat of the popped corn will melt the cheeses slightly. Leave the unpopped kernels at the bottom of the bowl.

BANANA BURGERS

The banana has been used as a food for thousands of years by people the world over. Some people even consider that it was a food in paradise, and that *is* a long time ago. Eat these hot with melted cheese in a toasted bun, with sauce or gravy, or cool them and serve them tomorrow in the lunch box. They may be frozen, cooked or uncooked. This recipe makes eight burgers. Allow 20 minutes to prepare and 20–30 minutes to cook.

> 2 ripe bananas
> 140ml (5fl oz) of water
> 55g (2oz) of finely ground nuts
> 55g (2oz) of sesame seeds
> 55g (2oz) of wheatgerm
>
> 55g (2oz) of wholewheat breadcrumbs
> 5ml (1 teaspoon) of ground cumin
> 5ml (1 teaspoon) of ground allspice

Mash the bananas into a bowl. Add the water and stir them together to an even consistency.

Mix the nuts, sesame seeds, wheatgerm and wholewheat breadcrumbs together in a mixing bowl.

Warm the oven to 190°C/375°F (Gas Mark 5).

Add the cumin and allspice to the dry mixture.

Stir the mashed banana in with the dry mixture using a large spoon.

Shape the moist 'dough' into patties, sausages or burgers and place on a baking tray.

Bake for 20–30 minutes at 190°C/375°F (Gas Mark 5). Serve immediately.

NUTS AND BOLTS

This is a novel way of serving healthy things to fussy kids. Decide what salad, dip or spread you will serve inside the 'nut'. Then use the 'bolt' to help push the food onto your fork. It takes only 20 minutes to prepare enough for 4 children. Idea: how many items can you see in your kitchen that make use of a nut and bolt to hold them together?

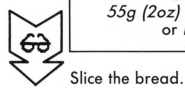

16 slices of wholewheat bread
55g (2oz) of margarine or *butter*

55g (2oz) of yeast extract
A biscuit cutter

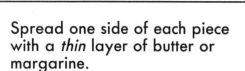

Slice the bread.	Spread one side of each piece with a *thin* layer of butter or margarine.
Warm the oven to 170°C/325°F (Gas Mark 3).	Spread the other side of each slice with a thin layer of yeast extract.
Press four slices together so that the butter sides face the yeast sides. Do this four times.	Divide sixteen by four ... Answer?
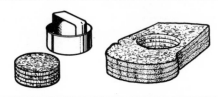	Use the biscuit cutter to cut a centre from each stack of bread slices: that leaves the 'nut'. The 'bolt' is the part which comes out *with* the biscuit cutter.

Place both the nuts and bolts on a baking tray and bake for 20 minutes at 170°C/325°F (Gas Mark 3). Remove them from the oven and fill the 'nut' with salad or dip.

9. DRINKS

CITRUS PUCKER

This blend of citrus juices tickles your tonsils and twists your whole face into an irresistible pucker. Use it to startle yourself into total wakefulness in the morning, or as a midday tonic for sluggishness. This will make enough for two and takes only 10 minutes to prepare.

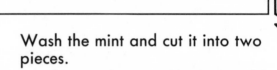

2 grapefruits	A sprig of fresh mint
2 large oranges	570ml (1 pint) of mineral water
2 lemons	A lemon press or juicer
(or 1 lemon and 1 lime)	

Slice the fruits in half.	Wash the mint and cut it into two pieces.
Squeeze the fruits and pour their juice into a large jug.	Pour the mineral water into the jug. Add the mint pieces.
	Stir the water and fruit juice together. Pour into two large tumblers and serve.

If this is really *too* puckery, try adding one teaspoon of honey to each serving — just to take the edge off.

APPLE JOLLY

The winters in some parts of the world are so cold that your breath can freeze as soon as it leaves your body: men with moustaches and children with runny noses grow pretty icicles on their upper lips. It's nice to have a warm drink waiting indoors to help lips and limbs thaw out, even if you haven't grown frosty. This will make enough for two adults and two children. It can be made in 20 minutes.

1 litre (approx. 2 pints)of apple juice *A 5cm (2 inch) piece of stick cinnamon*	*4 slices of lemon* *2 dried figs*

Pour the apple juice into a saucepan and place over a very low heat.

Place the cinnamon in the pan with the apple juice.

Wash and slice the lemon.

Wash and chop the figs and add them to the warm juice.

Leave the juice on the heat for 10 minutes at no more than a gentle simmer.

Place the lemon slices into four big mugs.

Strain the hot juice onto the lemon slices in each mug and serve immediately.

RHUBARB RAZZMATAZZ

Never mind the rhubarb, look at all those z's. Called 'zee', 'zed', 'zeta' and even 'izzard', z is often used to indicate bees, snoring, buzzers and zero. This is a simple to make showpiece for any party or gathering. Prepare most of it the night before you want it, the rest before serving — about an hour of your time in total. Serves 4 adults and 4 children.

900g (2lb) of fresh rhubarb stalks 3 litres (approx. 5 pints) of boiling water 16 slices of cucumber	8 slices of orange 8 slices of lemon 16 maraschino cherries 8 long cocktail spears Sparkling mineral water

	Wash the rhubarb very well.
Cut each stalk into 1.25cm ($\frac{1}{2}$ inch) chunks.	Place the chunks in a large enamel or earthenware bowl.
Pour the boiling water over the rhubarb and stir well.	Cover the bowl with a cloth.

Leave the rhubarb covered and undisturbed overnight.

Strain the liquid through a fine sieve into a large jug. Cover the jug and place it in the fridge to chill while you prepare the Razzmatazz.

	Wash the cucumber, orange, lemon and cocktail spears.
Slice the cucumber, orange and lemon.	Spoon the cherries into a bowl.
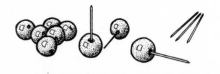	Push each cocktail spear through the centre of a cherry. Push the cherry right up towards the top of the spear.
Fold and spear a slice each of cucumber, orange, lemon and then another slice of cucumber.	
	Add another cherry to the bottom of the cocktail spear.

When all eight cocktail spears are prepared, place one in each of eight tall tumblers. Pour the chilled rhubarb juice over each and stir each serving once using the cocktail spear. Top up each tumbler with a splash of sparkling mineral water if desired and serve immediately.

SHORT, FAT AND SASSY

The servings are short and fat. The taste is sassy, which means bold or impudent (some *people* are like that). 'Sassy' also means a fruit preserve and there's that sort of sassiness in this beverage too. Serve as a starter or a nourishing snack. You will need 15 minutes to prepare enough for 2 adults and 2 children.

30ml (2 tablespoons) of grated creamed coconut 340g (12oz) of natural yogurt 285ml ($\frac{1}{2}$ pint) of cold milk (soya or cow's)	20ml (4 teaspoons) of celery seed 20ml (4 teaspoons) of honey or fruit preserves

Grate the creamed coconut.

Measure the yogurt and 285ml ($\frac{1}{2}$ pint) of milk into a jug. Stir to an even consistency.

Pour the milk and yogurt mixture into four short, fat tumblers. Sprinkle 7.5ml ($\frac{1}{2}$ tablespoon) of grated coconut onto each serving.

Sprinkle 5ml (1 teaspoon) of celery seed over each serving.

Spoon 5ml (1 teaspoon) of honey or fruit preserve onto each serving.

Give each serving a quick, vigorous stir so that the coconut, celery seed and honey or fruit preserve leave streaks in the yogurt and milk mixture. You may serve immediately or chill each portion for 30 minutes.

PEACH FURY

The beautiful flame colour of peaches lingers in this furious swirl of ingredients. Serve this drink icy cold with a spoon *and* a straw. It takes 15 minutes to make — but make it an hour before you want it. Serves 2 adults and 2 children.

A little boiling water	2.5ml ($\frac{1}{2}$ teaspoon) of ground cloves
4 ripe peaches	225g (8oz) of natural yogurt
570ml (1 pint) of apple juice	A food processor or blender

Bring some water to the boil in a small, deep saucepan.

Remove the stalks from the peaches.

Plunge each peach into the boiling water for 15 seconds. Remove, using a large slatted spoon, and peel the skin from the peach immediately.

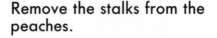

Slice the peeled peaches in half and remove the pip. Place the peach halves in the blender with the apple juice.

Purée the peaches with the apple juice until the consistency is even. Pour the mixture into four clear glasses and place them in your freezer compartment for one hour. The mixture should come nearly to the point of freezing.

Sprinkle a tiny amount of the ground cloves onto each portion.

Measure 55g (2oz) of yogurt onto each portion.

Stir quickly and *furiously* with a long thin spoon or knife.

Serve immediately.

ALLIGATOR WHIP

Do you know what the skin of an alligator looks like? Well, someone thought it looked like the skin of a certain sort of avocado — so they gave the avocado the name 'Alligator Pear'. I don't think I'd ever dare to whip an alligator but I *love* whipping avocados. This is very easy to digest. It takes only 10 mintues to make enough for 2 adults *or* 2 children. Idea: try growing an avocado tree from the stone. (Insert matchsticks or cocktail sticks in the stone to suspend it with the blunt end in water. Plant when rooted.)

1 large, ripe avocado *850ml (1½ pints) of milk* *(soya or cow's)* *10ml (2 teaspoons) of honey*	*10ml (2 teaspoons) of ground almonds* *(or other ground nuts)* *A food processor or blender*

Slice the avocado in half.	Remove the stone from the avocado.
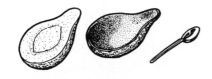	Scoop the 'flesh' from the avocado halves and place in the blender. Scrape right down to the skin — include the slightly brown flesh too.
Measure 850ml (1½ pints) of milk into the blender. Add 10ml (2 teaspoons) of honey and purée to an even consistency.	
Pour into tumblers.	Sprinkle each serving with 5ml (1 teaspoon) of ground nuts and serve immediately.

HERB SNUGGLES

These teas used to be called 'ptisans', then 'tisanes' — I just call them 'snuggles' because it's so nice to sit with one steaming its own distinct aroma. The secret of a good snuggle is to brew it as delicately as possible. That way the real essence of the herb is captured without a very bitter 'over-brewed' taste. These three potions are made using fresh herbs, if possible, and may be served chilled too. It is best to have a separate pot for making herb snuggles, as ordinary tea can leave a deposit in the pot. Each snuggle takes 10 minutes to prepare and serves 2 adults and 2 children.

MELISSA SNUGGLE: LEMON BALM
1 litre (approx. 2 pints) of water
Four 15cm (6 inch) sprigs of lemon balm herb
4 slices of lemon
Honey (optional)
*

GINGER MINT SNUGGLE: GARDEN MINT
1 litre (approx. 2 pints) of water
Four 15cm (6 inch) sprigs of garden mint herb

One 2.5cm(1 inch) piece of fresh ginger
Honey (optional)
*

CURLY ORANGE SNUGGLE: PARSLEY
1 litre (approx. 2 pints) of water
Eight 5cm (2 inch) sprigs of parsley herb
4 slices of orange
4 whole cloves
Honey (optional)
*

Boil the water.

Wash the sprigs of herb and pick off any brown parts.

Use 140ml ($\frac{1}{4}$ pint) of the boiled water to warm the tea pot.

Wash the lemon, ginger or orange. Slice the lemon or orange.